BEND IT LIKE BECKHAM

ein Film von Gurinder Chadha

von
Thomas Tepe
und
Gerda Piotrowiak

Ernst Klett Sprachen
Stuttgart

Kein Zweifel: *Bend it like Beckham* ist ein in besonderem Maße unterrichtsgeeigneter Film! Seine Charaktere und Themen, seine Handlung, Humor und Musik machen ihn zu einem höchst unterhaltsamen Film, der gleichzeitig durch die Kontrastierung zweier Familien und Protagonistinnen exemplarische Einblicke in die multikulturelle Gesellschaft Großbritanniens vermittelt. Auch filmtechnisch ist *Bend it like Beckham* ergiebig: Kameraführung, Schnitt, visuelle Symbole und gezielte musikalische Unterlegung machen ihn zu einem "well-made film", der bereits jetzt – auch unterstützt durch die gelungene Romanadaption (vgl. Klettbuch 578010) – ein moderner Unterrichtsklassiker insbesondere am Ende der Sekundarstufe I ist.

Der vorliegende Kopiervorlagenband ist als breites „Unterrichtsbuffet" konzipiert, aus dem sehr unterschiedliche Sequenzen gebildet werden können. Grundlage und Orientierungspunkt ist das Szenenprotokoll, das sich zwar auf die DVD bezieht, die dortigen *chapters* aber in kleinere Einheiten *(scenes)* zerlegt und diesen kurze inhaltliche Beschreibungen und Zeitangaben zuordnet. Nahezu alle folgenden Seiten sind als eigenständige Arbeitsblätter oder Folienvorlagen direkt kopierfähig: Sie verknüpfen oft unmittelbar Input mit Aufgabenstellungen und sind visuell ansprechend gestaltet.

Die Struktur des Bandes folgt dem klassischen *pre-/while-/post*-Schema und erlaubt die schnelle und flexible Zusammenstellung von „Unterrichtsmenüs" auf sehr unterschiedlichen Niveaus und mit variablen Schwerpunkten. Die Niveaukennzeichnungen *intermediate* und *advanced* (vgl. die Informationsleiste oben auf jeder Seite) lassen sich grob den Klassen 9/10 bzw. 11/12 zuordnen. Auch die drei Vorschläge zur schriftlichen Leistungsüberprüfung sind nach steigenden Anforderungen geordnet.

Die Bandbreite der Arbeitsblätter ist groß. Sie
- reicht von *film trivia* bis zu *film literacy*.
- ermöglicht die schrittweise Erarbeitung des Films, gibt aber auch Anregungen für offene, selbstgesteuerte Arbeitsformen.
- ermöglicht Filmkritik in sehr unterschiedlichen Textformaten.
- bietet für die Nachbereitung kurze nachbereitende schriftliche wie mündliche Übungen, erläutert aber auch komplexe Unterrichtsideen *(TV show, ideas for a sequel)* oder gibt Anregungen für den Vergleich mit Szenen aus anderen Filmen.

Bildnachweis

Pp. 3, 10–11: Foxsearchlight.com; p. 8: Cinetext, Frankfurt; p. 10: Cinetext, Frankfurt (Allstar / B Sky B); pp. 11, 16, 40, 41, 45, 46, 47, 49, 52: Ghetty Images PhotoDisc, Hamburg; pp. 13, 15, 17, 47: com!padres; pp. 21, 23: Clipart.com

The chapter divisions for this film vary between different DVD editions. For example, in the German version the film consists of 16 chapters (cf. chart below), but in the English version there are 20. The reason for this difference is that there is no universally accepted definition of how much material constitutes a chapter.
In order to enable teachers and students to pinpoint details, the following description is based on scenes composed of the smallest possible units, i.e. on parts of the film in which the action happens in one place. Two methods of editing are used in the film: the primary method used is one where the shots are arranged in chronological order, and the other, occasionally used method is montage editing, where a rapid alternation of juxtaposed or parallel scenes (e.g. wedding – finals) form longer sequences. This last editing method is indicated by an asterisk (*).There are no flashbacks.

Total running time: 01:41:40

Chapter	Scene	Content	running time
1	1	Opening credits; first commentary, then pictures of the match Manchester United vs. Anderlecht; Jess scores the decisive goal; interview in TV studio with football experts and Jess's mother; Mrs Bhamra barges into Jess's bedroom, switches off the TV set and tells Jess to come downstairs; before following her mother, Jess tells Beckham (= poster above her bed) that she is sick and tired of her sister's wedding; film title.	00:00:00
	2	Pinky tells her sister that she has to help her find a new outfit for her engagement party.	00:02:49
	3	Jess and Pinky are out shopping in Southall, where they meet their cousins Monica, Bubbly and Meena.	00:03:27
	4	Meanwhile Jules and her mother are looking at bras.	00:04:12
	5	Jess and Pinky meet Tony (Jess's best friend and school mate) and his mother and stop for a short chat.	00:05:01
2	6	Jess and her friends are playing football in the park; Jules watches them.	00:05:59
	7	Jess is in her bedroom talking to Beckham again when her father comes in and asks her to help him put up the lights for the wedding.	00:06:57
	8	Pinky's and Teetu's engagement party; Jess helps to serve the food.	00:07:58
	9	Jess's cousins are watching Jess and the boys play football in the park; they notice that Jules is watching Jess, too; Jules invites Jess to play for the Hounslow Harriers women's team.	00:09:26
3	10	Series of shots showing the Hounslow Harriers practice. Jess arrives at the football stadium to join a practice session; Joe, the coach, is very sceptical at first but asks her to come back when he has watched her play.	00:11:24
	11	Jess 'tells' Beckham about her trip to the stadium.	00:14:17
	12	Jules and her father are practising shooting goals in the garden; Jules is told off by her mother for taking so much interest in football.	00:14:52
	13	Football practice: Joe gives Jess some old football boots and a proper kit; Jess joins the other girls in the changing rooms, but stays behind when the warming-up begins; when Joe goes to her to find out why, he notices a scar on her leg; he shows her the scars on his knee and convinces her to join the others.	00:15:45
4	14	On her way home from the stadium Jess, still in her football kit, meets her friends in the park and starts playing with them. Mrs Bhamra sees them.	00:19:30
	15	At home her mother tells Jess off for not behaving properly. Jess tells her parents about the Hounslow Harriers, but they forbid her to join them.	00:20:16
	16	Jess complains to Tony about her parents' behaviour. He advises her to play secretly and Jules, who joins them, suggests a summer job as a good excuse. (airplane)	00:22:07

Chapter	Scene	Content	running time
5	17	Sequence of short scenes showing how Jess manages to get to practice with the Harriers without her parents knowing about it; she is shown on the pitch practising and taking part in a proper match. (no dialogue)	00:23:35
	18	(airplane) At Heathrow Airport Pinky is making love to Teetu in her car when her mother rings her and asks her to pick up Jess from work.	00:26:08
	19	In the Harriers' changing rooms Jess tells the other girls about her parents' expectations concerning picking the right partner.	00:27:01
	20	Jess arrives home to her mother's surprise without Pinky, who follows shortly afterwards. Jess has to confide to Pinky that she has joined a women's football team. A professional dress maker arrives to measure the girls for wedding outfits. Jess asks for money to buy shoes.	00:27:49
6	21	Sequence: shopping trip into Central London; Jess and Jules buy boots and shoes for Jess, have a drink in a pub and come home. (no dialogue)	00:30:24
	22	Jess returns home and her family discover that she has bought a pair of football boots.	00:31:27
	23	During the next football practice Jess tells Jules about her problems. Joe makes her run five extra laps as a form of playful punishment. She gets a cramp, but goes on running. He stops her, makes her sit down and massages her leg.	00:32:32
	24	Jess goes home with Jules to borrow a pair of shoes for the wedding and meets her mother.	00:34:41
	25	Jess and Jules are waiting at the bus stop, fooling about. Jules admits that she fancies Joe. Pinky's future parents-in-law drive past and watch the two girls.	00:37:12
7	26	Jess arrives home to find Pinky in tears because Teetu's parents have called off the wedding. They accuse Jess of having kissed an English boy in public. Jess manages to convince her parents that none of that is true, but then Pinky tells them that Jess has lied to them about playing football.	00:38:01
	27	Sequence: several short scenes without dialogue follow, Pinky is shown arguing with Teetu, sitting in her bedroom crying and being comforted by Jess.	00:40:19
	28	Joe asks Jules if she knows why Jess has missed two training lessons. She tells him about Jess's problem with her parents.	00:40:52
	29	Joe calls on the Bhamras to apologize for not having informed them about Jess playing for the Harriers. Mr Bhamra explains that he does not want Jess to be disappointed like he was as a young man. He was forced to give up cricket because of the colour of his skin / his religion. When Jess sees Joe out, he tells her that the team has been invited to play in Germany.	00:41:20
8	30	Sequence: trip to Hamburg Jess is the last to board the minibus that is taking the team to the airport. Her parents have been told that the two sisters are spending the weekend with a cousin. A number of short scenes follow showing the main stages of the trip leading up to the match against a German team. The Harriers lose because Jess misses a penalty.	00:43:33
	31	Back at home Mr Bhamra discovers that his daughters have lied to him when he sees a photo of the Harriers in Hamburg in the newspaper.	00:45:53
	32	After the match the girls plan to spend the evening at a club. Jess has not brought the right clothes, but is given a makeover by Mel, the captain of the team, and Jules.	00:46:23

Chapter	Scene	Content	running time
9	33	At the club Jess, who is not used to drinking alcohol, has some wine and dances with Jules and Joe. She feels dizzy, goes outside to get some fresh air and is followed by Joe, who grabs her arm when she stumbles. They are on the verge of kissing when Jules finds them and shouts at Jess.	00:47:00
	34	When the team arrive back in London, Jules storms out of the bus, not giving Jess a chance to talk to her. The Bhamras are waiting for Jess.	00:50:08
	35	Sequence: the Hamburg aftermath A number a short scenes follow showing Mr and Mrs Bhamra wondering what went wrong in their daughters' upbringing. Jess and her sister talk about love, and Pinky warns her not to get involved with an English boy. In two parallel scenes we see Jules and Jess both alone in their bedrooms, looking unhappy.	00:50:56
	36	Jess goes to explain her dilemma to Joe, who points out that she can't go on pleasing her parents forever.	00:52:43
10	37	Jess goes to Jules to apologize to her, but Jules does not accept her apology. Her mother hears bits of the girls' argument and draws the wrong conclusion. Sobbing, she tells her husband that Jules is a lesbian.	00:54:57
	38	Tony and Jess meet in a pavilion in the park. When Jess tells Tony that she needs an Indian boyfriend he tells her his secret that he is gay.	00:58:19
11	39	Sequence: With Pinky's help Jess manages to get away from home to play in the semi-finals. Tony and his friends come to watch the girls play. So does Mr Bhamra, who senses that his daughter has lied to him. He is impressed with Jess's talent. During the match, however, Jess is fouled and called names by another player. When she reacts aggressively, she is sent off the pitch. Back in the changing rooms Joe tells her off for risking the team's participation in the tournament. When he leaves, she runs after him. She is upset about his behaviour and starts crying. When he tries to console her and takes her in his arms, Mr Bhamra appears.	01:00:16
	40	Jess and her father arrive home to learn that Teetu's parents have come to apologize. When the Bhamras decide on a date for the wedding, they choose the day of the finals.	01:05:25
12	41	Joe and Jules are having an argument, during which she learns that a scout is coming to the finals.	01:08:00
	42	Jess is helping her father to put up the lights outside their house again when Jules arrives to tell her about the scout coming.	01:09:00
	43	At Jules's house her father is trying to explain the offside rule to his wife. She has decided to take more interest in her daughter's hobby. (airplane)	01:10:21
	44	The A-level results arrive. Jess has got the grades she needs to become a solicitor.	01:11:40
13	45	Sequence: A number a short scenes show the preparations for the finals and for the wedding: *– Jess hangs up some washing in the garden and then bends a ball around it* – Jules tells Joe that Jess won't be able to play *– Jess takes down Beckham's poster* *– wedding guests arrive at the Bhamras' house* – Harrier girls are practising for the finals.	01:13:08
	46	Joe arrives and watches the wedding party from outside. Mr Bhamra sees him and goes outside to talk to him. He tells him about the scout. Jess comes outside, too. She tells him about her exam results. He wants to know if she is engaged to one of the guests. They say goodbye and Jess returns to the party.	01:15:58

Chapter	Scene	Content	running time
14/15	47	Sequence / montage editing: the day of the wedding and of the finals: a number of short scenes are juxtaposed showing both events: – Jules and her parents leave the house to go to the finals *– the bride leaves her parents' house* – the Harrier girls are getting changed *– the wedding party is waiting for the bridegroom* – Joe is watching the girls warm up *– a meal is being served to the wedding guests* *– Tony suggests taking Jess to play in the second half and Mr Bhamra agrees* – Jess is getting changed while Tony is driving *– Pinky and Teetu are dancing* – Jess and Tony arrive at the stadium *– dancing at the wedding* – pictures of the match, the Harriers are losing *– Mrs Bhamra is looking for her daughter* – Jules scores a goal *– the wedding guests are dancing* – another player fouls Jess, there is a free kick – bird's eye view of the stadium, silence – when Jess looks at the goal keeper, she sees her sister and other members of the wedding party standing there – she kicks and scores a goal – Jess is lifted up by the other girls (climax) *– Pinky is lifted up by Teetu (climax)* – in the changing room the girls help Jess to change into her sari – Joe and the scout come to talk to Jules and Jess – Jules's parents watch the two girls embrace each other happily – on the way home Jules tells her parents about the scout's offer: a scholarship in Santa Clara *– back at the wedding, Jess joins in the dancing happily* – Jules's mother is sitting in the kitchen crying *– there is a fight at the wedding over the video*	01:19:21
16	48	The last part of the wedding ceremony: the bride is taking leave of her family. While this ceremony is taking place outside the Bhamras' house, Jules and her mother arrive. When Mrs Paxton notices that Jess is wearing her shoes, she accuses her of being a lesbian and forces her to take off the shoes. Jules drags her mother away. Pinky pulls Jess into the waiting car and asks for an explanation.	01:29:00
	49	In the car Jules explains that she and Jess both fancy the same man, their coach Joe.	01:30:46
	50	The family is relaxing after the wedding reception. Jess is unhappy because she can't tell her parents about the scout's offer. Tony tries to help her by announcing that he and Jess want to get engaged and get married after Jess has been to a college of her choice. But Jess is no longer willing to lie. She tells her parents about the finals and the scout's offer. Mr Bhamra explains that he does not want Jess to make the same mistake he made and therefore announces that they have no right to stop Jess from accepting the scholarship.	01:31:38
	51	Jess runs back to the stadium to tell Joe the good news. They embrace, but when he wants to kiss her, she shrinks back.	01:35:38
	52	Both families are waiting in the departure lounge at Heathrow Airport to see the girls off. Before they board the plane, Joe arrives and tells Jess that he is going to stay with the women's team and that he has told his father about his plans. He also asks Jess again if there is any chance of them getting together. When they finally kiss, David and Victoria Beckham appear in the distance surrounded by bodyguards.	01:37:32
	53	Sequence / parallel scenes show life at both girls' homes approximately 7 months later: – Jules's parents are opening a parcel from their daughter – Jess's mother is knitting baby boots because Pinky is pregnant – Mr Bhamra is playing cricket with Teetu and Joe	01:40:35
	54	Closing credits	01:41:40

1 If you have already seen the film, what do you remember about it?

2 Put the stills from "Bend it like Beckham" into the order in which they occur in the film and summarize the plot. Use the nine verb-noun phrases for your summary.

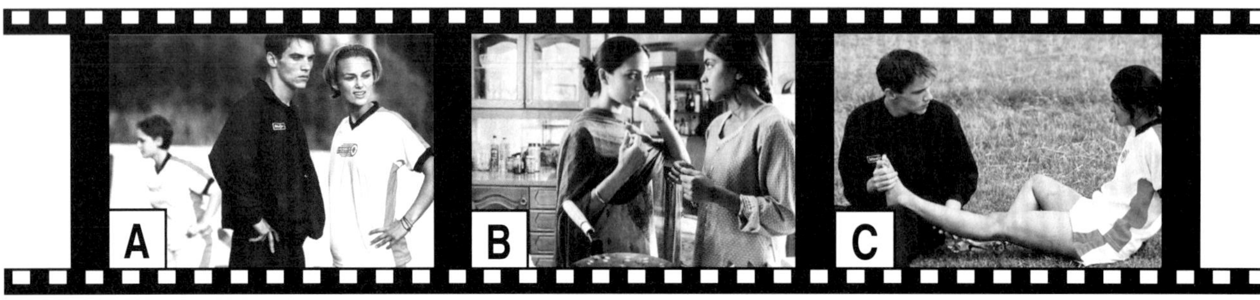

- **to realize a dream**
- **to jump to conclusions**
- **to face an embarrassing situation**
- **to give s.o. a scholarship**
- **to bring shame on s.o.**
- **to spoil / ruin an event**
- **to put the blame for s.th. on s.o. else**
- **to complain about s.o.'s behaviour**
- **to ask for s.o.'s blessing / permission**

1. Read the excerpts from interviews with the director/co-writer and with Keira Knightly. According to them, what makes this film such a great success?

2. What other reasons have made this film so successful?

3. In groups or in class, try to agree on the "top 5" reasons for the success of *Bend it like Beckham*. The vocabulary at the bottom of the page may be useful.

Director/Co-writer **Gurinder Chadha**

Bend It Like Beckham is my most autobiographical film. People think that must mean I wanted to be a professional football player (or 'soccer' as you crazy Yanks insist on calling it!). The truth is I was never into soccer growing up—it's only now after making the film that I can bend a ball almost as well as I can cook aloo gobi. […] I decided then to make a film combining the English passion for football with the Indian passion for marriage. Beckham scores a magnificent goal and rips his shirt off (my oh my…). When I get my breath back it dawns on me that Beckham's uncanny ability to 'bend' the ball around a wall of players into the goal is a great metaphor for what young girls (and film directors) go through. You see your goal, you know where you want to go, but you've got to twist and turn and bend the rules to get there.

Courtesy of FLM Magazine, Copyright 2002, Landmark Theatres

An extract from an interview with **Keira Knightly** (Jules)

Interviewer: Your director, Gurinder Chadha is known for being able to bring a natural, human feel to her films. She infuses them with a universal appeal.

Keira Knightly: They are very naturalistic tales in a heightened way. That's the reason that it [the film] is doing and will do so well in America. It's not as easy as baddies vs. goodies. You are able to form your own opinion and it's not like anyone has been preaching at you. She is so clever in doing that.

Printed by permission

excellent	skilful
extraordinary	exceptional
brilliant	unbeatable
fascinating	surprising
wonderful	unexpected
terrific	convincing
entertaining	humorous
original	unusual
plausible	unbelievable
realistic	fast-paced
effective	suspenseful
interesting	gripping
complex	…

Top 5

structure	editing
action	turning points
plot	moments
screenplay	ending
setting	dialogue
actors	humour
characters	effects
suspense	images
scenes	landscapes
emotions	storytelling
music	relationships
camerawork	…
message	

1. What information about the genre, the characters and the theme of the film do the posters give?

2. Who do you think is the target audience for the film?
   What elements do these posters include to attract the audience?

3. Which of the posters appeals more to you? Why?

Football

Did you know ...

... that Parminder Nagra (Jess) and Keira Knightly (Jules) had to undergo a two and a half month training period practising football together?

... that the Hounslow Harriers team doesn't exist, but almost all the players in the film are professional footballers?

... that Jess wears number 7 for the Hounslow Harriers, the same number David Beckham wears for England and once wore for Manchester United?

The Actresses

Did you know ...

... that Keira Knightly was captain of a girls' soccer team when she was eleven?

... that Parminder Nagra was worried that the scar on her leg would prevent her from getting the role of Jess? Instead, the scar – and the story behind it – were worked into the script.

... that although their characters are roughly the same age, in reality there is a 10-year age gap between Parminder Nagra (born 1975) and Kiera Knightly (born 1985)?

The Director & the Film

Did you know ...

... that Gurinder Chadha's relatively low budget independent film shot to number one in Britain in its first week of release and won the 'Best British Comedy Film' award of 2002?

... that raising the financial backing for *Bend It Like Beckham* was extremely difficult, partly because the leading actress is British Asian and not a star?

... that in the 1960s Gurinder Chadha's father came to London and was refused a job at Barclays Bank because he wore a turban, even though he worked for Barclays in Kenya?

... that *Bend It Like Beckham* is the third feature film from Gurinder Chadha? Her first feature film, *Bhaji on the Beach*, won numerous international awards, and the film What's Cooking was voted joint audience award winner of the New York Film Critic's 2000 season.

1 Which information do you find most interesting or most surprising?

2 Do research on the film using the internet and try to make up more of these "Did you know ...?" questions for your classmates. Further points of interest could be the film music or other characters (e.g. Jonathan Rhys Meyers, the "coach").

1 Here are ten facts about David Beckham. Match these headings with the information below.

Studying a star – Hard work – Favourite drinks
Fast ball – Promotion – Hard worker – New shoes
The red card – Top fan – Family man

1. Beckham admires the Brazilian player Ronaldo. After the World Cup game against Brazil, he asked Ronaldo to sign his shirt for Beckham's son Brooklyn.
2. David learned his football skills through hours of continuous practice and training. When he was younger, he practised mostly with his dad, but also on his own. His practice sessions took place in the local park and usually lasted until late in the evening.
3. On Saturday 22nd February 1997, David Beckham scored the equalising goal v Chelsea. The speed of the shot was measured at 157.5 kph.
4. David is married to Victoria, a former member of the pop group "The Spice Girls". He has Victoria's name tattooed on his arm in Hindi and the names of his first two children tattooed on his back.
5. Beckham says he is not a beer drinker, and that he prefers a decent glass of wine or Pepsi.
6. He was made captain of the England squad in November 2000 in a friendly match against Italy after serving as vice captain for the previous two internationals.
7. The study of Beckham is part of a 12-week "football culture" course at Staffordshire University.
8. Every game he plays, David wears a new pair of football boots, which cost approximately € 450.
9. An experiment at Manchester United showed that he runs an average of 14.2 kilometres per game – more than any other player on the team.
10. Beckham's behaviour on the football pitch is often unpredictable. He scores spectacular goals but also sometimes makes unfair tackles. At the World Cup in France in '98, an unfair tackle led to him being penalized.

2 What questions about Beckham are not answered in this fact file?

3 Try to answer these questions with the help of different sources of information.

4 Turn all the information into a humorous article on David Beckham.

1 Who does what?

People

coach / chairman
referee / linesman
crowd / spectators / supporters
(professional) players
goalkeeper / defender / marker / sweeper
mid-field player
attacker / forward / striker / winger
substitute (player)

Activities

to get support from s.o.
to break through the defence
to swap shirts
to be injured
to be suspended
to play up front
to dribble the ball past an opponent
to wear a football kit (shirt, shorts and socks)
to take part in a training session

to tug another player's shirt
to be offside
to book s.o. for an unfairness
to suspend s.o.
to send s.o. off the field
to sit on a bench
to show the yellow / red card
to protect / defend the goal
to shoot at the goal

to score a goal
to observe the game
to mark s.o. closely
to sit on the bench
to make up a team
to miss practice
to run laps
to wear a tracksuit
to sign s.o. on

2 Write the one-minute live radio commentary of the end of a football match.

Summary of the game:

- tournament / (quarter) final between … and …
- championship game (at home or away at…) / friendly match
- half-time / the first or second half of the game
- to be two goals down / to lead 1:0 / to be in the lead
- to play in (red) shirts and (blue) shorts
- penalty / own goal / equalizer

What is happening:

- to shrug off / outrun another player
- to tackle / foul an opponent
- kick / hit / stop / control / pass / bend a ball
- to have / maintain possession of the ball
- to do a double-step over the ball
- to volley the ball (into the net)
- receive / intercept a pass
- to pass forward / backward
- to be offside
- to make a header
- to get a free kick
- to beat / defeat s.o.
- victory / defeat / draw

All the British teen talk in the grid is used by the young characters in *Bend it like Beckham*.

1 Looking at the explanations, can you think of German teen talk expressions with a similar meaning?

British teen talk	Explanation	German
1. to sneak off	to go somewhere secretly	
2. to barge in (on s.o.)	to rudely interrupt s.th. / s.o.	
3. to send s.o. packing	to tell s.o. to leave at once	
4. to cover up for s.o.	to protect s.o. by hiding facts about them	
5. to shag s.o.	to have sex with s.o.	
6. to be starving	to be very hungry	
7. to pack s.th. in	to stop doing s.th.	
8. to have a fit	to be upset	
9. to rub s.th. in	to repeat s.th. too often	
10. to be mad on s.o.	to like s.o. very much	
11. to be mad at s.o.	to be angry at s.o.	
12. to fall for s.o.	to fall in love with s.o.	
13. to let s.o. down	to disappoint s.o.	
14. to be up to s.o. to do s.th.	to be responsible for s.th.	
15. to pick s.o. up	to go and get s.o.	
16. to put s.o. off s.th.	to make s.o. dislike s.th.	
17. to fix s.o. up with s.o. else	to find a partner for s.o.	
18. gorgeous	extremely attractive or enjoyable	
19. stressed out	unable to relax, under stress	
20. over the moon	very happy	
21. stunner	very attractive person	
22. fella	boyfriend	
23. bloke	man	
24. loo	toilet	
25. This *flipping* pen does not work!	These *adjectives* show that	
26. You *flaming* idiot!	you are angry and annoyed!	

2 Write one of the following using as many British teen talk expressions as possible:
a teenage diary entry – a letter to an agony aunt – a telephone conversation.

Fill in the gaps. The map and the picture will help you.

1. The capital of India is ____________________ .
2. In 1947, after 200 years of British rule, India became independent and was separated into two states, (Muslim) __________________________ in the north and (Hindu) India in the south. Unfortunately, this independence was accompanied by interreligious migration and widespread killings. Nehru became the first Prime Minister of India.
3. The conflict between Pakistan and India over the ____________________ region in the north of India has remained unresolved until today and has repeatedly led to military confrontations.
4. __________________ __________________, "the Great Soul", fought the British in a new way: non-violent non-cooperation. He was assassinated in 1948 by a Hindu fanatic.
5. The __________ _____________________ is one of the symbols of India. It was built in the 16th century.
6. Further symbols are the Indian flag and the __________________ flower.
7. The national currency is the Indian _______________.
8. With its population of 1,027,015,247 inhabitants (2001), India is the ____________________ most populous country in the world. However, 35% of the population lives below the poverty line.
9. Mumbai on the west coast is the centre of the Indian film industry. Its nickname 'Bollywood' is a combination of its former name __________________ and the American film metropolis 'Hollywood'.
10. There are 15 official languages in India and 844 different dialects. Hindi is the national language, but __________________ is the most important language for national, political and commercial communication.

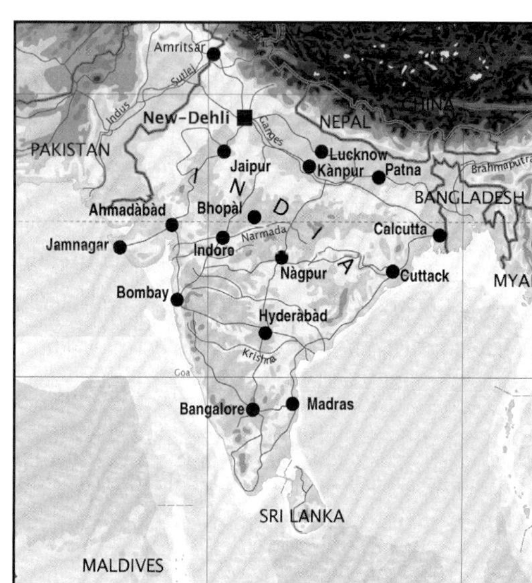

Solutions 1. Delhi – 2. Pakistan – 3. Kashmir – 4. Mahatma Gandhi – 5. Taj Mahal – 6. lotus – 7. rupee – 8. second – 9. Bombay – 10. English

1 Read the texts carefully and highlight arguments for and against arranged marriages.

Fact file: Arranged marriages

- Young Indian adults still let their parents find marriage partners for them and very rarely question this custom. Almost 95% of young Indian couples still get married in this way, with the full consensus of their families. Even among university graduates the arranged marriage is still the norm.

- It is the parents who select potential marriage partners for their children, considering their intellectual, cultural and social compatibility. The parents then introduce the couples. Accordingly, dating as a social practice is not common in India.
- Indians often point out that the divorce rate among arranged marriages is far lower than that of love marriages. They claim that in India marriage comes first, then love, whereas in a Western love relationship marriage often is the end of love.
- The wedding day is usually a big family celebration. Before and after the engagement, the couple is under close supervision to ensure that they don't sleep together before their wedding night.

Statement 1

"One of the biggest questions that I think people face with an arranged marriage is how in just a few meetings you will know that this is the person you want to spend the rest of your life with. I mean this is your life we are talking about."

Statement 2

"Marriage isn't on the top of my list at the moment, but I think it will be almost impossible to meet someone myself as I'm quite shy and busy studying. An assisted marriage, as arranged marriages are known as nowadays, would be a great way to meet someone from a similar cultural background who my parents would approve of. Basically, they would do the research into the family and if they like them they'd exchange photos. It would be up to me to decide if I like the guy and if I want to meet him. After the first date you are free to choose if you want to meet again. Although my parents would arrange the initial meeting, I don't feel much pressure from them as they prefer me to keep both doors open. If I was to meet someone myself then that would be fine but this way I have the back up. There is no pressure, as when I meet the guy it is totally up to me. I don't really believe in all this love at first sight crap and rather than falling in love before, you can fall in love gradually. My parents had an arranged marriage and they were dead against it at first, but once they met they quickly changed their minds and you can see that over the years they have grown much more affectionate towards one another."

2 Make a grid with the pros and cons of arranged marriages. Add further arguments not mentioned in the texts.

1 Examine the fact file on Sikhism. What makes it difficult / easy for Sikhs to integrate into British society?
What do you learn about the acceptance of Sikhs in British society?
What questions about Sikhs are not answered by the fact file?

Fact file: Sikhism

- Sikhism is a monotheistic religion that was founded in northern India in the 16th century by Guru Nanak (1469–1539). The Sikh religion today has a following of over 20 million people worldwide and is ranked as the world's 5th largest religion. 63% of the population in the Punjab, a province in the north of India, are Sikhs.

- Sikhism preaches a message of devotion to God, truthful living and the equality of men and women; it condemns superstitions and blind rituals such as fasting and visiting places of pilgrimage. A central part of Sikhism is the belief in reincarnation, which, however, is not used to justify the caste system, which they strongly reject.

- Sikh men often wear turbans and do not shave.

- "Saat Sri Akal" (Hindi) is a respectful traditional Sikh greeting meaning "Immortal God is Truth", spoken with one's hands clasped and one's head slightly bowed.

- Many of London's Sikh settlers arrived from the Punjab region of Northwest India during the 1920s, 1950s and 60s. Today Sikh people have played a significant role in numerous aspects of London life, including politics, the police force, education and sports.

- In the aftermath of 11 September 2001, there was a marked increase in the number of verbal and physical attacks on Sikhs wearing beards and turbans. It is thought many of these attacks happened because people mistook Sikhs for Muslims.

2 In Bend it like Beckham, Jesminder's family are part of a Sikh community in the west London suburb of Hounslow. What impression do you get of this Sikh family?

Film: ____________________ *Scene:* ____________________

Narrative techniques

Action

setting
time:
place:

plot

suspense
(unanswered questions)

Characters

appearance

body language
(face, gesture, movement)

use of language / communication

Main function of the scene:

Cinematic devices

Camera operations

Visual symbols

Film music / sound effects

Other effects

Narrative techniques

Step 1: First viewing – focus on action

→ *Try to understand the gist of the action, including key phrases of the dialogue.*

focus on action

setting: What is the time and place of action? What atmosphere is created?
plot: What happens and why?
suspense: What questions remain unanswered? Why do you want to keep on viewing?

Narrative techniques

Step 2: Second viewing – focus on characters

→ *Describe first, then comment on the impressions you get of the character(s).*

focus on characters

appearance: hair – cleanliness – clothes
body language: face – gestures – posture – movements
language / communication: choice of words – sentences – tone – interaction

Main function of the scene

Step 3: What is the main function of this scene in the film?

Put the scene into the context of the film. Does it move the action forward, build suspense, present a surprising turning-point in the action, reveal a new trait in the protagonist's character, introduce a new character, or define a relationship?

Cinematic devices

Step 4: Third viewing – focus on cinematic devices

→ *How do cinematic devices serve the main function of the scene?*

camera operations: camera operations – field size – movements – positions – angles

visual symbols (an object stands for s.th. else) → ***to visualise an idea or message***
Type 1: universally understood symbols (the American flag, the cross); Type 2: symbols which take on a meaning in the context of the film, e.g. through repetition or special emphasis (close-ups)

film music / sound → ***to show a mood or a character's emotions, to evoke nostalgic feelings for a past era, to foreshadow an event, to build suspense, to provide transitions between scenes, etc.***

montage, e.g.
- flashback → ***to provide background information, to recall a past event***
- flash-forward → ***to show future developments***
- cross-cutting → ***to show links between parallel events***
- jump cut → ***to cut out irrelevant action***

other effects, e.g.
- computer-generated imaging → ***to create realistic images, to turn artificial figures into convincing characters, to improve images, to create locations***
- slow motion → ***to intensify the moment, to underline effort or frustration***
- fast motion → ***to suggest superhuman speed / power***
- voice-over narration (voice speaking off-screen) → ***to give background information, to fill in gaps in the story, to reveal a character's thoughts, to convey the impression of a first-person or impersonal narrator***

Which emotions, attitudes or messages does the following body language reflect? If more than one interpretation is possible, describe the corresponding context or situation. Use the nouns in the box below. Feel free to use a monolingual dictionary.

Choice of nouns from A to Z

aggression • anger • anticipation • apprehension • authority • boredom • confidence • criticism defensiveness • dejection • delight • disappointment • disbelief • doubt • expectation • frustration impatience • indecision • innocence • insecurity • interest • nervousness • openness • pensiveness pleasure • readiness • rejection • relaxation • scepticism • sincerity • superiority • tiredness

Body language	Possible interpretation	
	nouns	*adjectives*
walking briskly and erectly		
standing with your hands on your hips		
sitting with your legs crossed, with your foot kicking	boredom	bored
arms crossed on your chest		
walking with your hands in your pockets, with your shoulders hunched		dejected
touching your cheek with your hand		
rubbing your eyes		
clasping your hands behind your back		
your head resting in your hand, with your eyes downcast		
rubbing your hands together		
sitting with your hands clasped behind your head, with your legs crossed		
showing your open palms		
tapping or drumming your fingers		
patting your hair		
having your head tilted		
stroking your chin		
looking down, your face turned away from your partner		
biting your nails		
pulling or tugging at your ear		

Use your notes and materials to make a 'viewing log' based on work in class and homework.
If you work in set groups during class, you can share your work and benefit from what other pupils find out.

Your log should include the following elements:

- a plot summary (cf. p. 41)
- profiles of the two main characters (protagonists) (cf. p. 43)
- a detailed analysis of one minor character, one theme and one analytic aspect (see examples below)
- profiles / detailed analyses of key scenes (cf. model scene profile and p. 18)
- a collection of memorable quotes (with context and comment) (cf. p. 42)
- stills (Use a search engine such as www.yahoo.com or www.google.com.) (cf. p. 8)
- your own review of the film (cf. p. 55)

The characters

Jess (Jesminder) Bhamra
Mr Bhamra
Mrs Bhamra
Pinky Bhamra (Jess's sister)
Jules (Juliette) Paxton
Alan Paxton
Paula Paxton
Joe (the coach)
Tony (Jess's friend)
Teetu – Pinky's fiancé

Themes

(women's) football
the generation gap
Indian culture and family life
conflicts
success and happiness
dreams and ambitions
expectations and wishes
tradition and change
love and friendship
marriage and religion
food and fashion
teenage talk

Analytic aspects

the constellation of characters
identifying with the characters
genre and humour
film music

Viewing log checklist

Student`s name:

		comments	*grades*
Formal aspects	cover table of contents structure / order / layout deadline met		
Contents	stills key scenes plot summary protagonists' character profiles quotes minor characters major theme analytic focus		
Review	**layout** **structure** – sequence of paragraphs **contents** – title, information, evaluation **language** – correctness, fluency, style		

Organize the project in 7 steps

Step 1: Introduce and explain …
- the project idea based on a topic chosen by the pupils
- the aims of the project
- the role of the teacher (project manager, adviser, "walking dictionary", etc.)
- the criteria for and methods of assessment.

Step 2: Suggest topics (see box below for examples). Hand out copymaster page 23 to help the pupils with their project. Ask them what additional aids they need to do their projects.

Step 3: Form groups of three to four pupils. Each group focuses on one topic.

Step 4: Write your timetable on a poster or transparency and explain it to the class. Here is a sample timetable:
- **Lessons 1–5**: viewing the whole film section by section in the first ca. 20–25 minutes of class, group sessions with discussion about notes.
- **Lessons 6–8**: group session, then plenary: interim reports / re-viewing selected scenes / organization / questions / … Plus individual work at home and additional group sessions in the afternoon as arranged at the end of each previous session. If needed, allow short periods of time at the beginning to discuss questions, matters of organization, etc. all groups are interested in. Set the dates for the presentations.
- **Lessons 9–11: presentations** (not more than 2 presentations per lesson)

Step 5: Carry out the project as planned.

Step 6: Assess the project in class. Use an evaluation sheet to prepare and structure this phase.

Step 7: Give individual grades for the students' participation and achievements in the project.

<table>
<tr><th>topics</th><th>copymasters (pages)</th><th>projects</th></tr>
<tr><td>Indian culture</td><td>16–17</td><td rowspan="10">fact sheet (1–2 pages)
+
15-minute group presentation
+
[chat show where a representative from each group participates]</td></tr>
<tr><td>football</td><td>12–13</td></tr>
<tr><td>conflicts</td><td>40–41</td></tr>
<tr><td>the main characters</td><td>43–46</td></tr>
<tr><td>love and friendship</td><td>32–33</td></tr>
<tr><td>techniques of filmmaking: genre, humour, music, camerawork, visual symbols, …</td><td>47–48</td></tr>
<tr><td>comparison of the novel and the film on the basis of selected scenes</td><td>50–51</td></tr>
<tr><td>our favourite film scene</td><td>18–20</td></tr>
<tr><td>additional materials on the DVD</td><td></td></tr>
<tr><td>…</td><td>…</td></tr>
</table>

During **group work** you are expected to ...

- act according to the role that you have been given
- refer to the topic and the task
- hand in work on time that completes the tasks
- listen attentively
- respect other opinions
- give feedback about the work of others
- contribute new ideas to the discussion

Presentations – Aspects for observation, feedback and assessment

content	description – analysis – comments
structure	introduction – transitions – conclusion / summary
media	functional use – management
voice	pronunciation – speed – volume – variation – emphasis – pauses
body language	facial expressions – gestures – posture
language	vocabulary – register – sentences – coherence – fluency – ...

Special tips for **group presentations**

- Before you begin, decide who is going to do what. Involve all group members in the presentation.
- Make sure that your presentation is well-structured and easy to follow. It is helpful to have a moderator, who is responsible for the introduction, the transitions between the various contributions and the conclusion.
- Rehearse your presentation. Improve your coordination between the parts of the presentation and manage your media effectively.

Only group members who play an active part should be "on stage".

Assessing the project – **key questions**

- Which new things did you learn?
- In what ways was working on a project different from other methods used in the classroom?
- Are you satisfied with your individual work, the work of other group members, the fact sheet and the presentation?
- Do you have any suggestions for improving the organisation and efficiency of the project?

Narrative techniques

Action

setting
time: the present
place: London, suburb of Hounslow,
Jesminder's bedroom in the attic, poster of Beckham over her bed, Manchester United Number 7 shirt
→ *importance of soccer in her life*

plot
Jess is in her bedroom watching a soccer match on TV (Man United vs. Anderlecht); the game is at a crucial stage; her wish to play for England becomes so strong that she sees herself scoring the deciding goal; she is interrupted by her mother, who turns off the TV set and sends her out shopping with her sister Pinky, whose engagement / wedding they are preparing for
→ *conflict dream – reality*

suspense
Will Jess be able to realize her dreams against all odds?

Characters

appearance
Jesminder (called Jess): long, dark hair tied in a ponytail, pretty, no make-up, blue tracksuit with a sleeveless top
→ *not interested in fashion*
Pinky: long dark hair, lots of make-up, tight jeans, red halter-neck top, sunglasses → *looks like any fashionable, young English woman*
Mrs Bhamra: bluish green shalwaar kameez and scarf
→ *traditional, conservative Indian* (cousins Meena, Bubbly, Monica: outfits similar to Pinky's) → *constellation of characters stresses that Jess is an outsider (isolation)*

body language
Jess keeps her hands in the pockets of her tracksuit top
→ *objection, protest*

use of language / communication
little meaningful communication, argument between mother and daughters, Jess "talks" to Beckham → *feels misunderstood by family; is isolated*

Main function of the scene:
Introduces the protagonist and her dilemma

Cinematic devices

Camera operations

Mainly medium and full shots, close-up / extreme close-up of Mrs Bhamra at the transition from dream to reality, in the scene in the TV studio she looks straight into the camera and tells Jess to come home, at home she bursts into her daughter's room → *distorted facial expression stresses how furious she is, the character of the mother is the main obstacle*

Close-up of David Beckham's smiling face (poster) after Jess has talked to him → *he is the incarnation of Jess's dreams*

Camera angles: camera not held straight when Hounslow High Street is shown → *conveys a lively, hectic atmosphere which is supported by the music*

Visual symbols

Football:
twice in the opening scenes of the film the viewer gets the impression that he/she is being hit by a ball
→ *strength, vigour (a sport generally associated with men)*

Music

fast, Asian-sounding tune when the two sisters are out shopping in Hounslow High Street
→ *underlines the multi-ethnic atmosphere created by a number of shots of market stalls, shops, customers, etc.*

Other effects

Computer generated imaging:
soccer match (Manchester United vs. Anderlecht) at the opening of the film is the original footage
until Jess scores the decisive goal, followed by
interviews with well-known soccer experts in the TV studio
→ *illusion of realism* until Mrs Bhamra is introduced → *underlines the intensity of Jess's dream*

Pre-viewing tasks

1. The German title of the film is "Kick It Like Beckham". Use your dictionary to explain the difference between the two verbs "bend" and "kick".
2. Consult a map of Greater London to locate Heathrow Airport, Hounslow, Southall. Try and find photos of Hounslow and Southall and use them to describe this part of London (e.g. use the Google search engine).

While-viewing tasks

1. Analyse how cinematic devices and narrative techniques are used to characterize the women you meet, i.e. Jess, her mother, her sister Pinky, her cousins Monica, Meena and Bubbly.
2. Describe the camera movements in the three different scenes. What is the connection between camera movement and setting?

Post-viewing task – writing a monologue

When Jess returns from her shopping trip with Pinky, she "tells" David Beckham about it. As we see in scene 2, she is very outspoken when she "talks" to her idol. Make sure what she says is in line with what we see in scenes 2 and 3.

Bridging the gap (→ scenes 4 to 8)

1. In scene 4 you will meet Jules (Juliet), another major character in the film. What are Jules and her mother arguing about?
2. Take notes on Jess so that you can produce a first character sketch at the end of scene 8.
3. Describe the rituals connected with an Indian engagement. Consider the following aspects: decorations, food, clothes, guests, presents.

Tasks: Solutions

Pre-viewing

1. to bend = to force s.th. into an angle or curve; to change direction to form an angle or curve; to kick = to hit s.th. with your foot; the first verb implies that greater skill is needed; not a straightforward movement
2. Hounslow and Southall are in West London and have a high percentage of Indian population; Heathrow = biggest of the London airports, international gateway to the USA, etc.

While-viewing

1. Cf. scene profile.
2. Cf. scene profile; in all the scenes inside (TV studio, the Bhamras' house) the camera is fairly static. When the sisters are outside in Southall High Street there are several shots from different angles underlining the idea of freedom and variety.

Post-viewing

Students are expected to use their knowledge of scenes 2 and 3. The way Jess has decorated her room reflects the fact that she is a football maniac. There are football shirts and there is a huge poster depicting David Beckham over her bed. Before Jess reluctantly leaves her room to go downstairs, she quickly tells Beckham that she "is sick and tired of this wedding" although it has not even started. When she is out shopping with Pinky, her body language reflects her lack of interest in fashion / make-up, etc.

Action

setting
time: a summer's day
place: a park
→ *perfect setting for leisure time activities and making new friends*

plot
Jess, Tony and some other Indian boys are playing football in the park. Jess is clearly the best player. (→ *Jess's skill is shown*)
Monica, Bubbly and Meena are watching them, admiring the boys' bodies. They notice that someone else is watching the group, too. Jules is sitting on a bench not far away. When the group stops playing, she walks across to them, introduces herself and invites Jess to come to a practice with her team, the Hounslow Harriers.

suspense
Is Jess talented enough to realize her dreams?
What influence will Jules have on Jess?
Will Jess accept Jules's invitation?
Will this new contact help her to achieve her dream?

Characters

appearance
Jess: tracksuit bottom and Manchester United T-shirt, hair tied in a ponytail, earrings but no make-up → *natural, not interested in her looks*
Monica, Bubbly, Meena: tight mini-skirts, T-shirts with plunging necklines, lots of make-up, sunglasses → *only interested in boys*
Jules: tall, slim, short fair hair, wears sports clothes → *casual, self-confident, not concerned about her looks*

body language
boys are fooling around, taking their shirts off to show off their muscles → *stereotypical butch image*
Jules and Jess shake hands → *new bond*

use of language / communication
Meena, Bubbly and Monica express their admiration in a very melodramatic way (extreme body language, squealing voices) → *exaggerated, artificial behaviour makes them ridiculous characters*
The boys make silly comments about women's football, which Jules just ignores → *Jules is self-confident, she knows what she wants*

Narrative techniques

Main function of the scene:
Shows the beginning of an unlikely friendship

Cinematic devices

Special camera operations
- long shot → *introduces the place of the action*
- full shots to show Jess's cousins and Jules both sitting in the park watching Jess and the boys play → *introduce the various observers of the game*
- tracking shot following Jess and the ball → *supports the idea of energy / life*
- over-the-shoulder-shot when Jules approaches Jess and her team → *camera adopts Jules's point of view, shows her as courageous, outgoing, communicative and confident*

Film music
very fast, rhythmic music when they play football
→ *stresses the speed of the game, underlines how fast and skilful Jess is (her energy and enthusiasm contrasts sharply with her behaviour at home)*

Other effects
contrast between
a) two groups of young people (players vs. observers)
b) Jess and Jules (in terms of appearance and ethnicity)
→ *makes a close bond between Jess and Jules unlikely until their shared interest in football is revealed*

Pre-viewing tasks

How much do you know about women's soccer?
Look at the following statements and decide if they are true or false.

a. In 1921 53,000 people attended a women's match played at the ground of Everton FC.
b. The first records of women playing football are frescoes found in China dating back to the 1st and 2nd centuries.
c. In 1955 the German Football Association imposed a ban on women's football.
d. In 1996 women's football was introduced at the Olympic Games.
e. In 2002 (when the film was released) there was no pro league in England for women.

While-viewing tasks

Teenage talk

1. You are going to watch a scene with lots of young people in it. Although they are roughly the same age, they have very different interests and are not all friends. You will hear the following 'names': slag – bitch – gori. In each case find out what the word means, who uses it and to whom it refers.
2. When Jules tells Jess about the Hounslow Harriers, Taz asks, "Do you swap shirts at the end of matches?" Explain the implications of this remark.

Post-viewing task – making a brochure

Jules says that the Hounslow Harriers "could do with some fresh blood". Imagine the club has launched a competition among its members asking them to design a brochure to attract new members. Get together in groups of 3 to 4 and collect ideas. Before you discuss the layout, brush up your knowledge on advertising.

Tasks: Solutions

Pre-viewing

All five statements are true. They can be used to start off a discussion about the recent boom in women's soccer, especially in Germany. The students should be given the chance to voice their opinions.

While-viewing

1. *Slag (offensive, suggests a lot of sexual partners): Jess to Bubbly; bitch (offensive): Bubbly to Jess; gori (offensive for a white woman): Monica about Jules.*
2. *Although he plays football with Jess, Taz is terribly prejudiced against women's soccer. This is revealed by his sexist comment.*

Narrative techniques

Action

setting

place: Hounslow Harriers' football ground, gasometers in the background → *realistic background / authenticity*
time: sunny afternoon

plot

Jess watches the Harriers' team practise before she actually approaches Jules and the coach Joe, who seems to be very sceptical. Although she has no proper boots, Joe lets her join in the game.
She plays so well and sets up goals for Jules that Joe is impressed. After the practice he asks her about her parents' attitude to football and Jess lies, pretending that it is all right with them.
Thus Joe asks her to come back.

suspense

Will Joe accept her?
Is she good enough for the team?
What will her parents say when they hear about Joe's offer?
Will she tell them about it?

Characters

appearance

Joe: in his twenties, tall, very slim, wears a blue track suit
→ *attractive white male*
Jules: white football dress, hairband keeps her hair out of her face
→ *professional, relaxed*
Jess: dark hair tied in a ponytail, blue track suit, red Manchester United shirt underneath
→ *dressed for the occasion, professional; shows openly which club she supports*

body language

Joe and Jules communicate in a non-verbal way: e.g. Joe raises his thumb to show that he is impressed by Jess → *strong bond between Joe and Jules, intimacy*
Joe raises his eyebrows when Jess says she has not got any football boots, rolls his eyes upwards → *shows his sceptical attitude to Jess openly*
Jules puts arm around Jess's shoulder → *friendship, support, protection*

use of language / communication

Joe talks to Jules in a very playful tone when he explains that she started the team → *sign of affection, familiarity, friendship*

Main function of the scene:
Shows the protagonist pass the first test on her path to her dream and hints at new complications

Cinematic devices

Camera operations

- Crane shot at the beginning: girls practising
  → *gives overview, shows the atmosphere*
- Close-up of Jess, who is watching the team with bright eyes
  → *fascination, eagerness to join*
- Close-up of Jules and Joe talking about Jess
  → *stresses their close relationship, shows Jess as an outsider*

Visual symbols

- Warm colours of a golden sunset at the end of the scene when the three J's are leaving the pitch
  → *indicates harmony / mutual sympathy*
- Shadows → *foreshadow complications in this triangular relationship (eternal triangle)*

Other effects

Editing: very fast cuts at the opening of the scene showing the Harriers practising → *stresses their skills and their energy*

Music

Song "Do your thing":
very fast music every time you see the girls play football
→ *underlines their strength, vigour, speed*

Pre-viewing task

What are the qualities of a good coach? In groups of 3 or 4 discuss what you expect from a good coach. Make a list with qualities you consider important. Put them into a hierarchical order.

While-viewing tasks

1. Concentrate on Joe and his behaviour as a coach. Would you call him a good coach?
2. Study Joe's body language. Explain what it reveals about his attitude towards Jess.

Post-viewing task – writing an interior monologue

Jesminder takes part in her first football practice. What is she thinking?

1. Look at the following adjectives and choose five that Jess might use to describe the situation and her feelings.

mean	narrow-minded	determined	silly	aggressive	happy
nervous	exciting	different	shy	friendly	scared

2. Write an interior monologue using some of the chosen adjectives.

Bridging the gap (→ scenes 11 to 26)

1. After her first enthusiasm Jess does not want to take part in her first proper practice. Explain why.
2. How does Jess overcome her parents' objections to her playing for the Harriers?
3. Characterize Pinky. What are her ambitions in life and how does she achieve them?
4. Describe Jules's influence on Jess.

Tasks: Solutions

While-viewing

1. Students could apply the criteria they set up in the pre-viewing activity. Depending on their results there, they might point out that Joe seems to be strict, critical and observant, but does not treat all the members of his team the same. Jules plays a special part although she is not the captain (privileged treatment).
2. Cf. scene profile.

Narrative techniques

Action

setting
time: in the afternoon
place: a) 21 bus stop, b) living room
→ *exemplifies Jess's life outside and inside her family*

plot
Jess and Jules are laughing about Jules's mum, having a good time and are half-hugging each other when Teetu's parents drive past and misinterpret the situation. When Jess comes home, Pinky's future parents-in-law are in the living room, talking to Jess´s parents. Pinky is standing in the kitchen entrance, crying. Her future mother-in-law is angry, holding Jess's parents responsible ("Children are a map of their parents."), her husband a little apologetic. After they have left, Pinky shouts at Jess, making her responsible for her wedding having been called off. Jess explains what really happened. Her mother understands and takes her side ("We´re never good enough for them.") Then Pinky tells her parents about Jess playing in a football team.

suspense
Jess's parents are under pressure by the Indian community: will they ever allow Jess to play football like any English girl? Will they become even stricter now?

Characters

appearance
Jules: short blond hair, leather jacket, jeans;
Jess: jeans jacket, long black hair tied to a plait, jeans
→ *they both look like "typical" English teenagers*
Pinky: bright green T-shirt, jeans
→ *looks more Indian than Jess*

body language
e.g. Jess and Jules (at the bus stop):
giggling, fooling around, being childish, hugging each other
→ *shows their friendship and the similarities between them*
e.g. Jess in the living room, just standing / looking at the others
→ *seems absolutely surprised / dumbfounded*

use of language / communication
Jess and Jules: talking excitedly about Joe, laughing
→ *relaxed atmosphere*
Pinky (at home): swearing, crying, shouting → *anger, frustration*
Jess defends herself, swears on Babaji → *her voice reflects her desperation*
Jess's crying mother → *overly emotional (element of humour)*

Main function of the scene:
Shows how the protagonist's two worlds collide

Cinematic devices

Camera operations

- Establishing shots
  → *introduce the bus stop scene and the two arguments*
- Point of view perspectives in the living room
  → *to depict the arguments between the two families and Jess's inner conflict from both perspectives*
- Close-up of Pinky
  → *underlines the state she is in*

Visual symbols

- Different styles of clothing
  → *indicate two contrasting worlds (Turban, scarf versus the denim jacket)*
- The Indian family in a Jaguar (British higher class status symbol)
  → *suggests a process of assimilation and growing prosperity*

Film music

- Background song in the living room
  → *stresses the disappointment and grief of the parents and Pinky*
- Hindi version of the song
  → *alienating effect, one of the numerous hints that we are living in a multicultural society, but also a funny element, which makes the situation less tense for the viewer*

Other effects

- Contrasting scenes in terms of atmosphere and tone
- Mix of two different languages spoken at home
  → *Jess lives within two different cultures*

Pre-viewing task

When two people who are members of the Roman Catholic Church or the Church of England plan to get married, the marriage banns are read in their relevant parish churches on three successive Sundays. This is done to make sure that there is no "impediment" to the marriage. Find out what kind of "impediments" there are.

Post-viewing activity – writing a dialogue

As usual Pinky and Teetu meet in her car at lunch-time. Write down the dialogue they might have after the wedding has been called off. Make sure that it is very emotional.

Bridging the gap (→ scenes 27 to 32)

1. Why does Joe suddenly turn up at Jess's house?
2. When Joe calls on the Bhamras we find out why Jess's father objects so much to his daughter playing football. Explain what happened to him when he was young.
3. Why is Jess able to take part in the trip to Hamburg after all?
4. Describe the atmosphere during the team's stay in Hamburg.
5. How does Mr Bhamra find out that Jess has gone to Hamburg with the Harriers?
6. What part does Jess play in the match against the German team?

Pre-viewing tasks: Solutions

In the Roman Catholic Church there are three kinds of impediments:

1. consanguinity = people who are related by blood or descended from a common ancestor,

2. affinity = a relationship between persons which results from a valid marriage, e. g. a man cannot marry his mother-in-law,

3. previous marriage

Useful source: Catholic Home Study Service, http://www.cin.org

Narrative techniques

Action

setting
time: the present, at night
place: a) Hamburg, in front of the hotel,
b) inside and outside a Hamburg night club
→ *in a foreign country, outside the control of the parents: the ideal location for romance*

plot
Joe is waiting with the rest of the team when Jess and Jules come out of the hotel to join them. Joe is fascinated by Jess´s looks. In the club: Joe is sitting on a sofa, Jules sits down beside him. Jess joins them.
Jules wants to get Joe away from Jess, so she asks him to dance. They dance mechanically, there is no emotional connection. Jess finally follows them onto the dance floor. Joe dances with Jess and ignores Jules, so Jules tries to separate them by dancing between them. Jess soon feels dizzy (alcohol) and walks out to get some fresh air. Joe follows her and helps her walk by putting his arm around her. Jess says how much she admires him for talking to her parents.They are about to kiss each other for the first time when Jules sees them and calls Jess a "bitch!".

suspense
Will the rivalry between the girls be stronger than their friendship? Will Jess lose her best friend? Will she give up Joe?

Characters

appearance
Jess: wears her hair loose, tight black dress, make-up
→ *urprisingly attractive, even sexy; has adjusted to the Western concept of femininity and beauty*
Jules: bright top (bare shoulders and back) → *seductive, very sexy*
Joe: black shirt and trousers → *smartly dressed, handsome*

body language
Jess: smiles at Joe, can't walk steadily → *slightly tipsy, unaware of her attraction, flirtatious*
Jules: dances frantically, grim and tense facial expression, pushy → *tries to get between Jess and Joe and to draw Joe's attention towards her, shows her feelings for Joe openly*
Joe: looks at Jess while dancing, touches his heart, holds her hand → *is obviously more attracted by Jess than by Jules, offers her help and thus grasps the opportunity to be alone with her*

use of language / communication
Jules: makes Joe dance with her although he doesn't want to → *obtrusive towards Joe, forces herself upon him, insensitive*
Jess and Jules: reluctantly talk about more personal things, but do not put their feelings into words → *get gradually closer to each other ("love is in the air", cf. the romantic setting)*

Main function of the scene:
Shows the protagonist facing a new conflict, i.e. forbidden love vs. friendship

Cinematic devices

Camera operations
Mainly medium shots; two close-ups at the beginning of the scene: Jess appears at the entrance of the hotel (tilt up) and Joe catches sight of her → *suggests that s.th. is going to happen (foreshadowing) between the two;* establishing shot of the night club and the terrace outside → *sets the scene for romance*

Visual symbols
the hotel with all its comfort → *Jess is entirely part of the Western world that night*
the colours of Jess and Jules's clothes do not match, Jules is the odd one out → *signals their disharmony that night, foreshadows conflicting interests and different strategies, indicates Jess's superiority*

Other effects
Lighting: flickering lights of the dance floor inside the club
→ *situation is tense, confusion (reflects the emotional turmoil of the protagonists); in comparison, the light outside on the terrace is warm and relaxing (contrast) and underpins the romantic moment*

Film music
Song 'I turn to you' → *love song whose lyrics reflect the message conveyed by the protagonists' body language*

Pre-viewing task

Listen to the song "I turn to you".

1) Who is the speaker?
2) Who is being addressed?
3) If you think about the main characters in "Bend it like Beckham", who could "turn to" whom in what situation?
   *Note: The lyrics are available at http://www.lyricsdownload.com

Post-viewing activity – writing a letter

Imagine you are Jules. Write a letter to Jess after the incident in Hamburg.

Bridging the gap (→ scenes 24 to 49)

1. Jess goes to Jules's house to apologize, but this visit leads to further complications. Explain why.
2. What does Jess find out when she asks Tony for help?
3. Sum up what happens in the semi-final.
4. Things begin to look brighter for Pinky and Jules. Explain why.
5. Look at the notes you took about Indian engagement parties while watching scenes 4 to 8. Now add information about weddings.

Tasks: Solutions

Pre-viewing

1. *A young woman in love / a young woman who has realized that she is in love / a female speaker who wants to be with somebody: she knows for sure that she has found the right one, the one to be with.*
2. *The unknown lover / everybody who is listening to that song, because especially young listeners can easily identify with the speaker / singer and make up their own addressee in their mind.*
3. *Jess confesses to Joe that she's in love with him. / Jess and Joe dance with each other for the whole night and are visibly in love with each other. / Joe feels attracted to Jess, tries to catch her attention as much as possible and finally wins her heart. / Joe tells Jess that he has fallen in love with her, they kiss, but then Jess runs away. / Joe tells Jess he is in love with her, but Jess doesn't want to know anything about it because Jules has just told her that she has a crush on Joe.*

Post-viewing

In her letter to Jess Jules expresses her disappointment and anger:

- *Jules probably accuses Jess of having exploited their friendship in order to get closer to Joe.*
- *She might also reproach Jess for having known about Jules's affection for Joe and for being inconsiderate or even unscrupulous.*
- *Jules may call Jess names and may swear at her.*
- *She may even threaten Jess.*

Action

setting
time: the present
places: in front of the Bhamras' house / in a ballroom / on the football pitch

plot
While Pinky is enjoying her wedding party / celebrations, Jess keeps on thinking about the final of the football tournament. The match is important because a talent scout from America is watching it. Finally Jess´s father allows her to go and play, "if that is the only way to make her smile". She plays and scores the decisive goal.

suspense
Will Jess and Pinky realize their very different dreams?

Narrative techniques

Characters

appearance
Jess: hair and face made up, sari in pink and gold → *looks like a traditional Indian girl*; later: in football kit → *looks like a professional football player*
Pinky: also dressed in a sari, lots of jewellery (gold), typical Indian make-up → *looks like a traditional Indian bride*

body language
happy and smiling faces at the wedding: Jess tries to smile → *accepts the importance of the day/wedding, pretends to enjoy the festivities*; players on football pitch and Joe with sad faces and resigned postures → *they´re one-nil down and face a defeat*; at the end of the scene everyone's body language *expresses joy, jubilation and victory*

use of language / communication
Mostly celebrations with almost no meaningful dialogue except when Jess's father gives Jess permission to leave the wedding → *key moment: her father can't stand Jess's unhappiness any longer and makes this decision without having consulted his wife, thus presenting himself as a truly loving father*

Main function of the scene:
Demonstrates that a "bridging" of cultures is possible

Camera operations

Cinematic devices

- Mix of establishing shots, medium shots and full shots → *portray the atmosphere in the ballroom and on the pitch*
- close-ups of faces → *present the mood of the people (joy or sadness, approval or disapproval), e.g. Jess's guilty conscience when suddenly her mother, sister, and aunts appear as a defensive wall in her mind*
- tracking shot of the ball → *follows its movement, takes the viewer very close to the action*
- many cuts (pictures and music are getting faster, too) → *fast-paced action; creation of suspense*
- extreme close-up of the ball → *to make the viewer feel close to the object*

Visual symbols

(Ride in the) car: Tony takes Jess to the football match while Jess is changing in the car (from sari into football kit) → *Jess is on her way from one culture to another, from sadness to happiness; the ride in the car stands for the transition from one world to another one (changing clothes = changing identities); Tony serves as a mediator between the two worlds*

The plane: it is just taking off from nearby Heathrow Airport (as shown again and again in different scenes) → *symbolizes Jess´s way into a new life; foreshadows her flight to America ("escape route from home")*

Film music / sound effects

beginning of the scene.:
pop music ("Inner Smile" by Texas) → *symbol of British culture*
followed by music by a Bhangra band, which is a mixture of traditional Indian music (written in the Punjabi language) and contemporary musical styles like disco, techno, house, rap, etc. → *symbol of the symbiosis of two cultures*
end of the scene:
classical music – Nessun Dorma from Puccini's opera "Turandot" preceded by silence and the sound of the wind → *the goal corresponds with the climax of the aria, which creates deep emotions within the viewer*

Other effects

editing:
cross-cutting from wedding ceremony and football match → *to show the parallel action of events: both girls are happy and their dreams and wishes are fulfilled at the same time*
slow motion:
following the ball → *creation of suspense: Will Jess be able to "Bend it like Beckham"?*

Pre-viewing task

Watch the scene until Tony suddenly turns up at the wedding.
What do you expect will happen?

While-viewing activities

(can be prepared as split-viewing tasks in 4 groups)

1. Silent viewing or freeze frame:
   - Why does Tony turn up?
   - What are Tony, Jess and her father talking about? Write down what they might say.
2. Focus on action / plot development:
   Analyse the setting and the atmosphere. How is suspense created?
3. Focus on characters:
   Examine the use of contrast in the outward appearance and explain its function.
4. Focus on film technique:
   Show the connection between the camera operations and the music.

Post-viewing activities – researching an opera

Explain the choice of music and its function.
Find out about the plot of Turandot. Are there any parallels between the opera and the film?

Bridging the gap (→ scenes 48 to 49)

1. On the DVD the following scenes are referred to as "The shoe shocker". Explain why.
2. Contrast Pinky's and Jess's ambitions.

Tasks: Solutions

Pre-viewing

- *Jess's father and Tony might have an argument*
- *situation escalates, wedding might be disturbed*
- *Jess might be "punished" by her father*

While-viewing

Cf. scene profile.

Post-viewing

Choice of music and its function:
pop song "Inner Smile"; aria "Nessun Dorma" from Puccini's opera "Turandot"; Bhangra music
→ symbiosis of different cultures

Narrative techniques

Action

setting
place: the Bhamras' house, kitchen and living room
time: after the wedding

plot
The family is relaxing after the wedding reception. Jess is unhappy because she does not know how to tell her parents about the scout's offer. Tony tries to help her by announcing that he and Jess want to get married after Jess has been to a college of her choice. But Jess is no longer willing to lie. She tells her parents about the final and the scholarship she has been offered. Mr Bhamra explains that he does not want her to make the same mistake he made. He feels he has no right to stop Jess and thus agrees to let her go.
→ *conflict between secrets / lies and the truth (honesty is rewarded)*

suspense
At the beginning: Will Jess choose the easy way out and play along with Tony's lie? How will Mr Bhamra react to his daughter's confession?
At the end: Is this the happy end or will further complications arise?

Characters

appearance
Jess, Mrs Bhamra, Tony's mother, Biji: festive saris, wedding outfit, different shades of red / orange / pink
Cousins: silk tops, halter neck
Mr Bhamra: white shirt, turban
Tony: dark brown shirt and tie with matching trousers
→ *adequately dressed for the wedding in a variety of styles, thus meeting the demands of the formal occasion (adaptation to expectations / social norms)*

body language
E.g. Mrs Bhamra, Tony's mother, Biji: sitting on sofa, feet put up on table in front of them → *relaxed, just listening, passive observers*
speakers: standing in front of the fireplace → *at the centre of attention*
Jess: tears are running down her cheeks when her father speaks
→ *tears of joy / relief*
Etc.

use of language / communication
sequence of three surprising announcements / speeches by Tony, Jess and Mr Bhamra mixed with exclamations of surprise / joy
→ *show Tony's supportiveness, Jess's honest confession and Mr Bhamra's acceptance of his daughter's right of self-determination in a sequence of unexpected twists in the action*

Main function of the scene:

Shows the protagonist come of age and how her honesty and courage help her achieve her dream

Cinematic devices

Camera operations

Field sizes:
combination of full shots, medium shots and close-ups, medium shots and close-ups predominate → *put stress on speakers' and audience's reactions*
Camera angles:
high-angle and low-angle shots → *camera assumes the characters' points of view (speaker standing – main audience sitting)*
Camera movement:
it zooms in on faces and away from them again, otherwise fairly static → *the messages of the speakers are the focus of a scene with little physical movement*

Visual symbols

glass of whisky: Mr Bhamra pours himself a drink before he explains that he does not want Jess to give up her dream as he did → *alcohol as a means of plucking up courage / of calming down / of bearing the tension*

Music

Hindi tune when Jess embraces her father at the end → *happy ending is in line with, and reaffirms their common family values; letting Jess go strengthens the unity of the family*

While-viewing tasks

Images only:

Watch the scene with the sound switched off. Examine the action carefully, paying special attention to camera movement and body language. Then make some inspired guesses to answer the following questions:

a. What are Mrs Bhamra, Biji and Tony's mother talking about at the beginning of the scene?

b. Judging from the family's reaction, what might be the message of
   - Tony's speech?
   - Jess's speech?

Take notes. Then watch the scene again, this time with the sound switched on.

Post-viewing task – comparing two scenes

In this scene Mr Bhamra pours himself a strong drink (whisky / brandy?) before he explains why he feels he has to let Jess go. There is an earlier scene in the film in which alcohol plays an important role. Compare the two scenes and explain what they have in common.

Bridging the gap (→ scene 51)

1. How does Joe react when Jess tells him her good news?
2. The scene bears parallels to an earlier scene. Say which one. What is the difference?

Tasks: Solutions

While-viewing

The scene lends itself to this kind of exercise because there is very little action and the camera operations will help the students to guess what is going on.

a. The three women have taken their shoes off and have put their feet up. The scene opens with a close-up of their feet. They are talking about Mrs Paxton wondering why she wanted Jess to take her shoes off.

b. Tony: Tony takes Jess's hand and drags her into the living room. Both are standing in front of the fireplace. Whatever it is Tony is saying seems to be difficult for him. When Tony has finished talking, Mr Bhamra is the first to jump to his feet to shake hands. His mother embraces him. Students might guess that he said he would like to marry Jess.

Jess: She makes a long speech. The tension shows on her face. But there is also an occasional smile. She seems to be very determined. Her mother seems to be shocked by what Jess says. This might lead students to the conclusion that she is asking her parents to let her go to America.

Post-viewing

After the match in Germany the team goes to a night club to relax. Jess, who does not seem to be used to drinking alcohol, has two glasses of wine, which make her feel dizzy. When she goes outside to get some fresh air, Joe follows her and catches her when she stumbles. The wine seems to help Jess to open up and shed her inhibitions. She almost kisses Joe. Students should discuss this presentation of the use of alcohol critically.

Narrative techniques

Action

setting
place: Heathrow Airport, departure lounge
time: present, sunny summer's day

plot
The Paxtons and the Bhamras have come to the airport to see their daughters off. When they are getting ready to go through passport control, Joe arrives. Jess runs back to him and learns that the Hounslow Harriers are going to play professionally and that Joe is going to coach them. Thrilled by the good news, Jess forgets about her family. When Jess's and Joe's lips touch, there is a scream from Jules because in a glassed-in corridor above them David Beckham appears, accompanied by his wife and bodyguards. Jess just turns around briefly. She promises Joe to talk to her parents when she comes home at Christmas.

epilogue (approx. 7 months later)
The Paxtons open a present from Jules; Pinky is pregnant; Mr Bhamra is playing cricket with Joe and Teetu → *cross-cultural harmony*

Characters

appearance
Jess: red top, brown skirt, trainers, hair loose, earrings
→ *attractive, feminine (new confidence)*
Jules: black leather jacket, blue jeans
→ *confident (as usual)*
Mrs Bhamra: pale apricot shalwar kameez
→ *traditional clothes*
Mrs Paxton: white trousers, black and white blouse with low neck, sunglasses
→ *stylish, fashionable (outward contrast to Mrs Bhamra)*

body language
Mr Paxton and Mr Bhamra shake hands
→ *friendship, reconciliation*
Mrs Bhamra offers Mrs Paxton a hanky to dry her tears
→ *united in grief*

use of language / communication
Jules: exclamations of joy, surprise when she opens her mother's present and when she sees Beckham
→ *her excitement contrasts with Jess's quiet joy*

Main function of the scene:

Dénouement and epilogue:
The protagonist finds happiness in her love life.
Harmony is all around.

Cinematic devices

Camera operations

Over-the-shoulder shots and close-ups of Jess and Joe
→ *camera assumes the point of view of each of the lovers in turn, enables the audience to identify with them, shows that the rest of the world is not important for them*
At the end of the main film, still / freeze of Jess and Jules waving good-bye to their families → *memorable happy ending; "full stop" for the main story: dividing line between two stages in their lives*
Zooming-out at the end of scene 53 → *smooth transition, in line with atmosphere*

Visual symbols

Plane: at the opening of the scene a plane can be seen again → *freedom, escape, fulfilment of dreams*
David Beckham: Jess's role model appears at the airport as she is about to leave; she turns around to look at him, but stays in Joe's arms → *idol has lost its appeal, it has been replaced by a real live man*
Playing cricket: in the epilogue, Mr Bhamra is shown playing cricket with Joe and Teetu → *assimilation, integration into British society*

Film music

Song "Inner Smile" when Jess and Jules kiss; song "Move on up" when Jules and Jess walk through passport control → *lyrics reflect the action*

Other effects

Cliffhanger: Jess's and Joe's budding romance rouses new interest in the audience → *new suspense, room for speculation*

Pre-viewing tasks

1. Look up the terms "epilogue" and "cliffhanger". Compare them and explain what they might have in common.
2. Explain the following two proverbs:
   – Out of sight, out of mind.
   – Absence makes the heart grow fonder.
   Which of them do you agree with? Give reasons.

While-viewing tasks

1. Stop the film after scene 52 (still of Jules and Jess waving goodbye).
   Comment on the effect this scene has on you. Would the term "cliffhanger" be suitable here?
   Explain why / why not.
2. Speculate about Jess's and Joe's relationship. Will it last?

Post-viewing tasks – discussion and letter-writing

1. Comment on the effect scene 53 has on you. Do you think it should have been omitted?
2. Letters from America: Having been at St Clara for two weeks, the girls write home. Write these letters for them.
   Make sure what you say is in line with what we know about the respective characters. You have a choice:
   – Jess writes to her parents / to Joe / to Tony.
   – Jules writes to her parents.

Tasks: Solutions

Pre-viewing

Epilogue = concluding section of a literary work, in which it is revealed what happened to the characters after the denouement; It is also used to refer to a short speech delivered at the end of a play and to the moral of a fable
Cliffhanger = situation in a story, film / movie, etc. that is very exciting because you cannot guess what will happen next, or you do not find out immediately what will happen next, very common in soaps

Post-viewing

1. Students might argue that the epilogue is too exaggerated, making the ending too happy and thus completely unrealistic.
2. Individual answers.

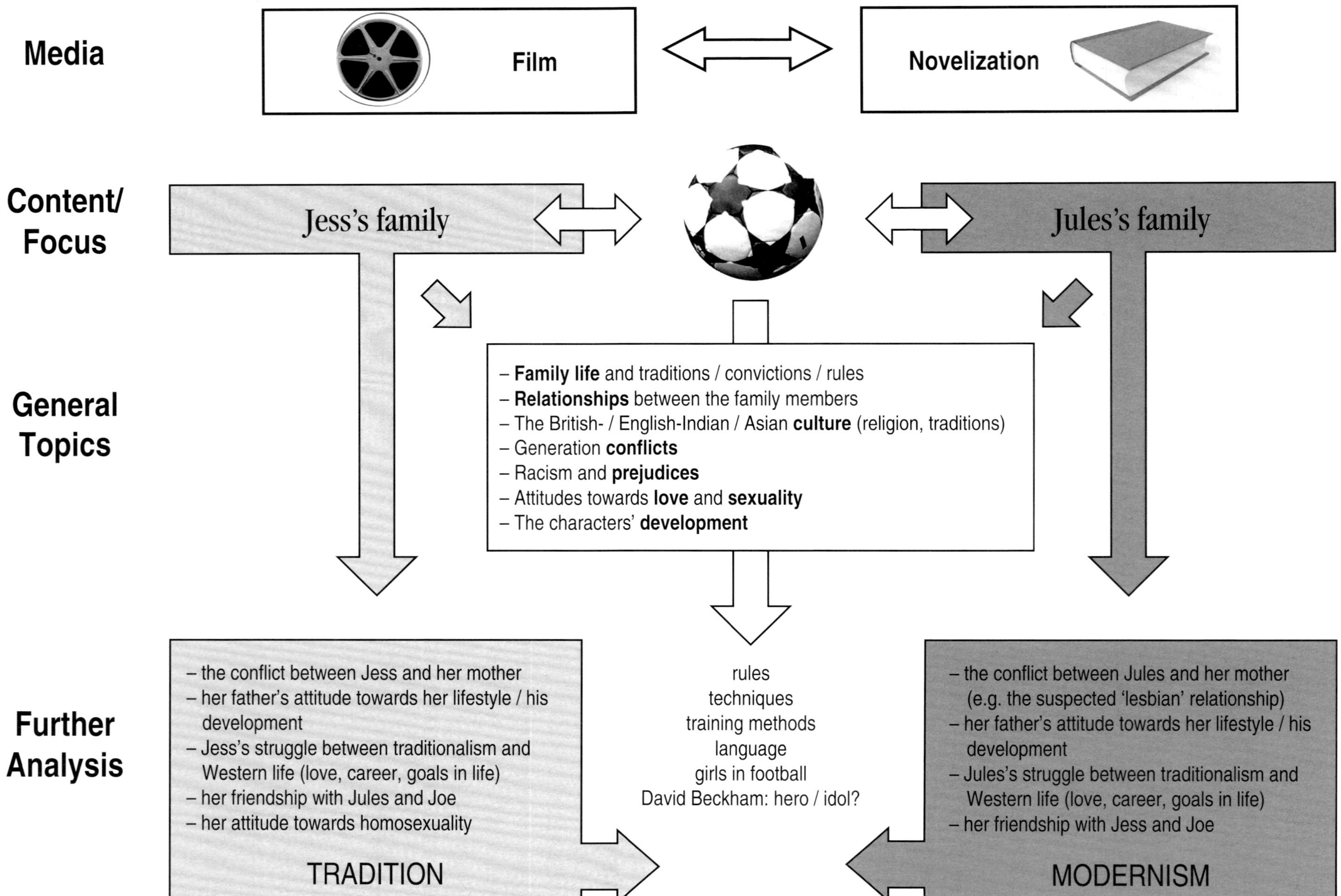
Media
Film
Novelization
Content/ Focus
Jess's family
Jules's family
General Topics
– **Family life** and traditions / convictions / rules
– **Relationships** between the family members
– The British- / English-Indian / Asian **culture** (religion, traditions)
– Generation **conflicts**
– Racism and **prejudices**
– Attitudes towards **love** and **sexuality**
– The characters' **development**
Further Analysis
– the conflict between Jess and her mother
– her father's attitude towards her lifestyle / his development
– Jess's struggle between traditionalism and Western life (love, career, goals in life)
– her friendship with Jules and Joe
– her attitude towards homosexuality
TRADITION
rules
techniques
training methods
language
girls in football
David Beckham: hero / idol?
– the conflict between Jules and her mother (e.g. the suspected 'lesbian' relationship)
– her father's attitude towards her lifestyle / his development
– Jules's struggle between traditionalism and Western life (love, career, goals in life)
– her friendship with Jess and Joe
MODERNISM

Plot the sequence of events in a film, novel or play, arranged in a way that shows not only what happens, but also the reasons for and links between these occurrences (causality).

1 Understanding **reasons**: answer these why-questions about the film, then formulate your own questions about the characters' behaviour.
Why is it unrealistic that Jess will realize her dream?
Why is Jess ashamed of wearing football shorts?
Why is Pinky's wedding nearly called off?
Why does Jules feel so bad after the trip to Germany?
Why is the final so important for Jess and Jules?
Why does Jess's father allow her to leave her sister's wedding in order to play in the final?

2 Discuss possible **alternative developments** of the plot. How likely or logical would they have been in the context of the film? Practise the if-sentences type III.
What ***would have happened*** if one of the characters ***had behaved*** differently?

3 The film uses a number of **conflicts** to create and maintain suspense. There is a conflict between the main character and her overprotective family, a conflict between British and Indian cultures, etc. Add some more conflicts. Think also of internal conflicts or conflicts of interests and expectations. Are all these conflicts resolved at the end of the film? Do racism and stereotypes play a role in the film?

How to write a **plot summary** of a film

1. Briefly describe the setting and the characters, then say what happens and how the events are logically connected.
2. Base your summary on the film: this is not the place for interpretation, analysis or personal comments.
3. Avoid direct speech.
4. Use the present tense.
5. As far as possible, use your own words.
6. Make use of connectors to show how the events are connected:
   - At the beginning (of ...)
   - Then / Later / Afterwards ...
   - Therefore / For this reason ...
   - As a result / Consequently ...
   - While ... / In the meantime ...
   - Finally / In the end / At last ...

1 Write a faulty **plot summary** of the film *Bend it like Beckham* with exactly five mistakes. Let someone else find and correct the mistakes.

2 You may also try to summarize the plot of this film in the form of a "**mini-saga**", i.e. a story which is exactly 50 words long.

3 Get into groups of seven, sit in a circle and write a seven-sentence "**snowball summary**":
- Write the first sentence of your plot summary on a sheet of paper.
- Pass your sheet to your right-hand neighbour.
- Write the second sentence of the summary that you have received from your left-hand neighbour. Then pass it on again to your right-hand neighbour.
- Continue in this way to build up seven different summaries in your group.
- At the end of the exercise you get back the summary which you started and which is now complete. Share and discuss the summaries in your group. Choose the best one and present it to the class.

Who speaks to whom in which situation? Fill in this grid. What else do you remember about the context of the quote?
Do you remember any other memorable quotes?

10 memorable quotes	spoken by	in this situation
1. You can't plan who you fall for. It just happens. I mean, look at … Posh and Becks.		
2. I was eight. My mum was working overtime at Heathrow. And I was trying to cook beans on toast. And I jumped up to the grill to get the toast. And my trousers caught light so my sister put me in the bath, poured cold water over me and pulled them off. And half my skin came off too … it put me off beans on toast for life.		
3. Don't tell me. The offside rule is when the French mustard has to be between the teriyaki sauce and the sea salt.		
4. She fouled you. She tugged your shirt. You just overreacted, that's all.		
5. Our designs will make even these little mosquito bites look like juicy, juicy mangos!		
6. Just because I wear trackies and play sports does not make me a lesbian!		
7. Anyone can cook aloo gobi, but who can bend a ball like Beckham?		
8. Losing to the Jerries on penalties comes natural to you English. You're part of tradition now!		
9. You're jumping to all the wrong conclusions!		
10. At least I taught her full Indian dinner, the rest is up to God.		

1. Tony to Jess	shortly before admitting his homosexuality („Posh and Becks" = Victoria and David Beckham)
2. Jess to Joe	explaining the scar on her leg
3. Paula Paxton to her husband Alan	after accepting her daughter's football enthusiasm, she asks Alan to explain the offside rule during a meal
4. Joe to Jess	explaining how he saw the situation before Jess was shown the red card, not knowing that she was called „Paki" by an opponent
5. dressmaker to Jess	commenting on Jessminder's breasts when taking her measurements for a dress to wear at her sister's wedding
6. Jules to her mother	reacting to her mother's suspicion that Jules is not interested in boys
7. Jess to Tony	expressing her frustration over the conflict between her parents' expectations and her own dream
8. Joe to Jess	after Jess missed a penalty when playing a German team in Hamburg („Jerries" is an informal expression for the Germans)
9. Alan Paxton to his wife Paula	responding to her theory that their daughter must be a lesbian because she is only interested in football and has no boyfriend
10. Mrs Bhamra to her husband	after having agreed to let Jess go to the US

Make a one-page character profile for a character of your choice. You may structure it like shown above.

Physical appearance

Name

Characteristic quotation

Family
(social background)

Personality / Character traits

Short biography

Relationship to other characters

Place the character on this scale.

flat, "stereotypical" character:
one-dimensional / describable in one sentence
predictable / static

round character:
complex / lifelike
surprises / develops and learns

He / She personifies / represents / portrays
(e.g. a certain part of / group in British society, an attitude or value system)

complexity scale

1 Arrange the characters of *Bend it like Beckham* on this **complexity scale**.

flat, "stereotypical" character:	**round character:**
one-dimensional	develops and learns
describable in one sentence	complex
predictable	lifelike
static	surprises

mood/success chart

2 A **chart** illustrates a character's development, e.g. in terms of changes of mood or degrees of success.

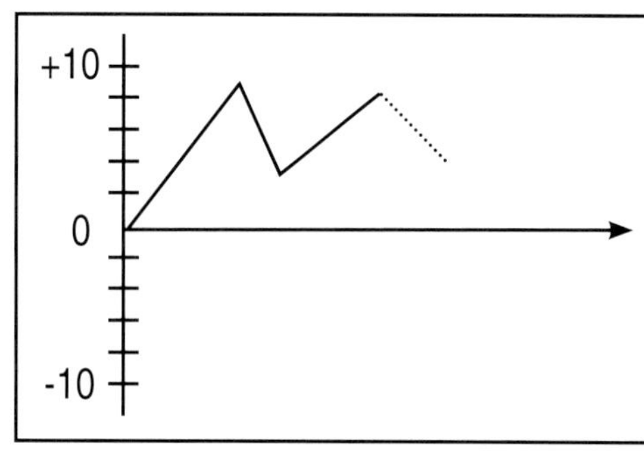

Here are the steps for how to make a **mood chart**:

Step 1: Draw a horizontal line starting at zero to mark the beginning of the story. This is the line on which you will mark major story events. Then draw a vertical line through zero with a scale from +10 (very positive feelings) to -10 (very negative feelings). This is the line that indicates each character's feelings in reaction to these events.

Step 2: As you follow the plot, mark important events on the chart according to each character's state of mind at the time. Work from left to right.

Step 3: Connect the marks in a line to show the ups and downs experienced by each character.
Tip: For comparison, draw mood curves for the two or three main characters on the same chart.

Step 4: Collect adjectives which describe different moods, e.g. aggressive, angry, anxious, calm, carefree, ... Use the words and the curve to explain each character's development.

cast of characters

3 Present the **cast of characters** in a film / novel / play on one page.

Tips: You can indicate the following aspects:

- the **importance** of characters (main vs. minor characters) by the letter size and position of the names on the page.
- the **closeness or distance** of the relationship of the characters by the length and thickness of the connecting lines (very close – close – friendly – superficial – hostile)
- the **type** of relationship by symbols, e.g. ⚭ (married), ☺ (friends), ...

4 Compare your solution with the presentation of characters on page 45.

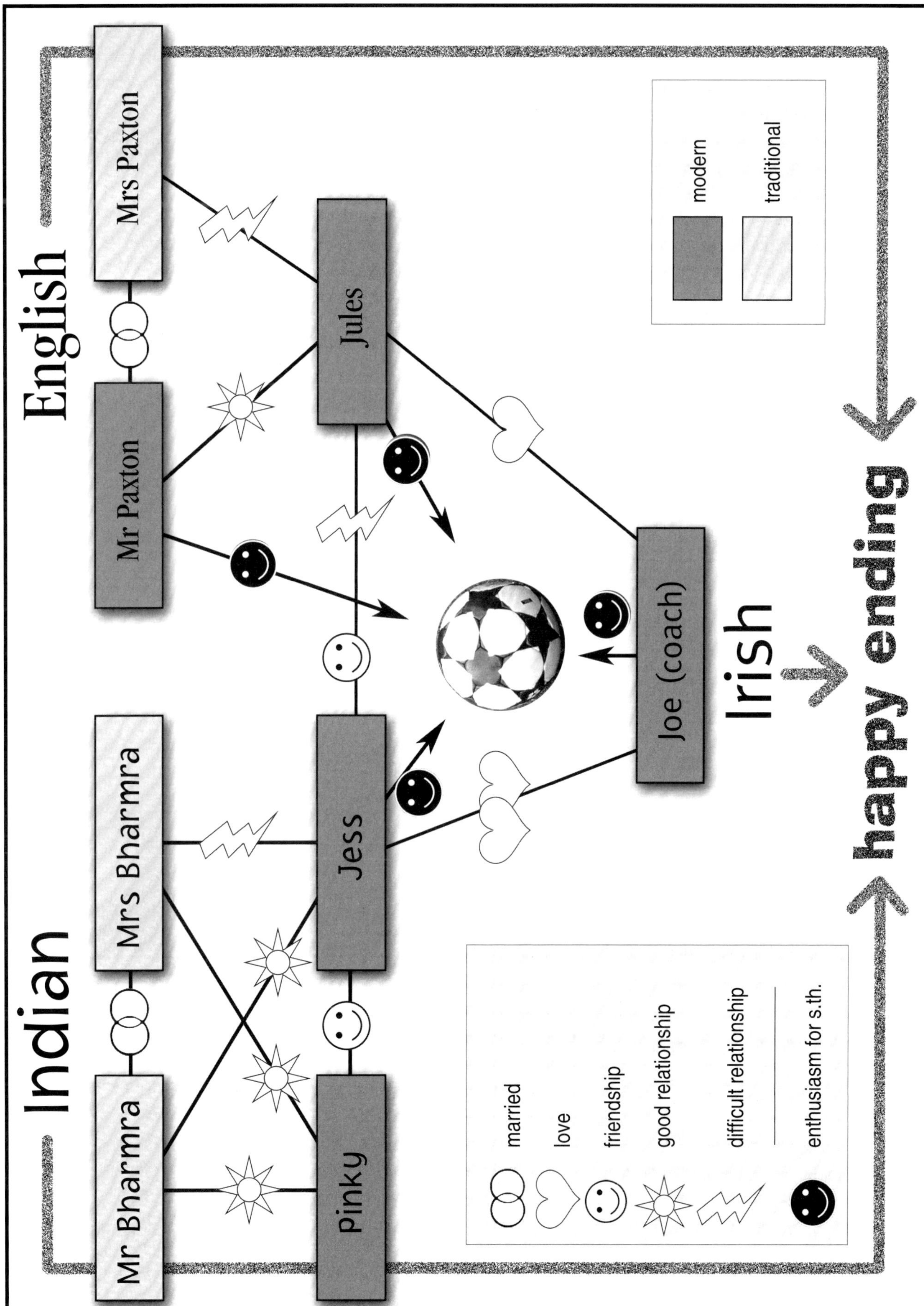
English
Mrs Paxton
Mr Paxton
Jules
Indian
Mrs Bharmra
Mr Bharmra
Jess
Pinky
Irish
Joe (coach)
happy ending
modern
traditional
married
love
friendship
good relationship
difficult relationship
enthusiasm for s.th.

the viewer

loves / hates / understands ...
identifies with ...
suffers with ...
sympathizes with ...
empathizes with ...

emotional identification
(audience empathy)

... are role models /
identification figures for ...

the film characters

are shown in conflicts or crisis situations
face danger, unkindness, humiliation, insecurity, ...
experience ups and downs / successes and failures in life

1. Explain the phrase "audience empathy" with the help of the chart above
2. How important is it to create audience empathy in a film? Consider different genres and target groups.
3. How important is the creation of audience empathy for the success of *Bend it like Beckham*? Discuss this question in class or write a fictitious interview with the director.

genre

1. Match the kinds of film (genres) with the correct topics / keywords.

action
adventure
comedy
drama
fantasy
horror
mystery
romance
teen movie
science fiction
thriller
sports movie
western

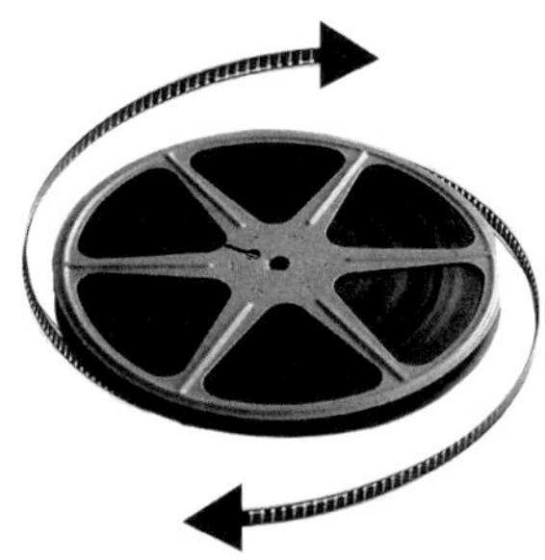

cowboys and Indians
dangerous, exciting, unusual experiences
strange, shocking events
events set in the future
exciting story of a crime or murder
love story
unrealistic story with fairytale elements
fast-paced, suspenseful plot
unexplainable events
teenagers' experiences
crises or conflicts in people's lives
events which make viewers laugh
crises / conflicts in the world of sport

2. Which genre do you think *Bend it like Beckham* belongs to? Why? (You may also suggest a combination of genres.)

3. Which target audience is the film aimed at? Describe it in terms of gender, age and interests.

4. "Bollywood" is a term used to describe the popular films produced in India. The name comes from combining Hollywood and Bombay, the city which is the centre of the Indian film industry.

Bollywood films are usually a mixture of colourful romance, comedy and family drama, with sometimes up to a dozen musical sequences.

To what extent is *Bend it like Beckham* a Bollywood film?

humour

5. How is humour created in *Bend it like Beckham*?

Examples of devices that create humorous effects:

- **stereotypical or "flat" characters**, i.e. characters who can be described in one phrase and who do not change or learn,
- **jokes** told by a character (to make fun of s.th., to mock s.th.),
- absurd or unrealistic **situations** with strange or extreme behaviour, confusion or misunderstandings, funny contrasts (e.g. in characters' appearance or behaviour) or stereotypical views.

1. The Indian music in *Bend it like Beckham* is called "bhangra pop". It sounds like Jamaican reggae played on traditional Indian instruments. In general, when are Indian and western pop music mixed in the film *Bend it like Beckham*? Why do you think this is done?

2. With the help of this grid, analyse the function of the western pop songs in the film. How do they fit the situations? What themes do they express?

Useful vocabulary

- Music may be: melodious / catchy / rhythmic / guitar-based / repetitive / monotonous / …
- The mood is / the lyrics are sad / melancholic / relaxing / moving / romantic / joyful / …
- The song has a catchy melody / an easy-to-remember refrain / a repetitive beat / a simple rhythm / …

song list in chronological order	scene	description (instruments, mood, ...); key phrases from the lyrics – relevance for the scene(s) in which they are played
She's a Lady *(Austin Howard)*	Hounslow Harriers football training montage, after Jess and Joe talk about their scars	
Move on up *(Curtis Mayfield)*	when Jess is sneaking off to matches and training while the family thinks she is at work; when Jess is training with veggies in the kitchen; saying good-bye at the airport; end sequence	
The Power of Love *(Amar; originally by Jennifer Rush)*	Pinky and Teetu in the car when Pinky gets the call to pick up Jess from work; after the wedding has been called off	
Independence Day *(Melanie C)*	Jess and Jules are downtown shopping for shoes	
I Turn To You *(Melanie C)*	at the club in Hamburg	
I Wish *(Victoria Beckham)*	playing in the Hamburg club when Jess and Joe go out on the terrace	
IOU = I Owe You *(Victoria Beckham)*	in the background on the kitchen radio when Jess visits Jules after Hamburg	
Red Alert *(Basement Jaxx)*	Jess sneaking off to play while Pinky & parents go to the Temple	
Dream the Dream *(Shaznay Lewis)*	after Jess gets her A-level results; hanging washing in the garden	
Inner Smile *(Texas)*	on the wedding day; Jess kissing Joe at the airport; seeing David Beckham	
Hot Hot Hot *(Bina Mistry)*	sung in Hindi with the closing credits, with the cast and crew singing along	

Letters

1. Jess and Jules have left for the US. Now write a letter to one of the main characters in the novel. Comment freely on his or her actions, decisions and motives and give him / her advice on how to behave in the future.
2. Pretend you are Jesminder. Write her letters to David Beckham a) at the beginning of the film and b) after she has been in America for several months.
3. Pretend that you are Jules. Write the letter that she would send to an agony aunt after returning home from Hamburg.
4. Write Mrs Parker's letter to a psychologist at the beginning of the film, in which she complains about her daughter's unusual hobby and seeks professional advice. Let another student answer this letter.

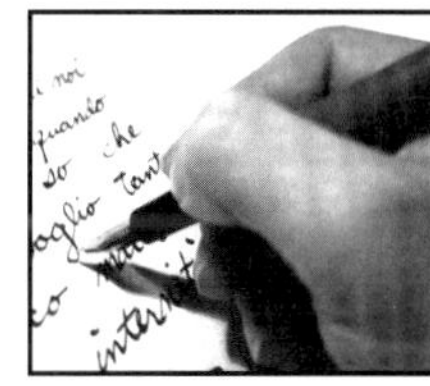

Stories

5. Turn the film into a ***long short story*** with different parts, each describing a key scene from the film. Start with the first meeting between Jess and Jules. Write your story from a third-person neutral perspective or the first-person perspective. Compare the different versions.
6. A ***mini-saga*** is a story which is exactly 50 words long. Its title may be between 1 and 15 words long. Rewrite the plot of the film as a mini-saga.

Article

7. Write a newspaper article for a British popular newspaper entitled "Two local girls signed on by American soccer club." Feel free to do any of the following:
   - dramatize events by exaggeration, sensationalism and speculation; personalize the story by highlighting individual experiences and feelings (focus on "human interest"),
   - include half-truths and gossip as well as quotations from various people,
   - use everyday, informal language.

Interview

8. A reporter interviews a character after the end of the film (e.g. Mr Bharmra).
   Use as many of these nine verb-noun collocations as possible during the interview:

to lead to a crisis / to be confronted with rules and restrictions / to solve a problem to experience a difficult or an embarrassing situation / to meet someone's expectations to overcome difficulties / to provoke a conflict / to avoid an open confrontation / to cope with a dilemma

Dialogue

9. Write a dialogue between neighbours of the Bhamra family who have observed the events of the film and have very different views on what has happened.

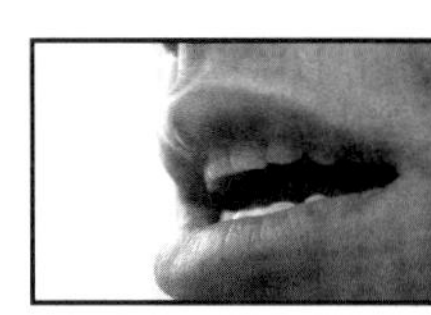

Hot chair

10. In groups, prepare questions for the main and some of the minor characters of the film which can be answered on the basis of what happens in the film.
    - Focus on expectations and reactions: *Why do / does … ask / help / invite / teach / expect / tell / want + somebody (not) to do s.th.?*
    - Explore alternative behaviour: *What do you think would have happened if you had (done) …?*
    - Look towards the future: *If you met / saw / could decide …, (what) would you …?*

    Then some students take the "hot chairs" and answer the questions while playing the roles of the film characters.

Before you view / read

1. Who do you think reads novelizations, and why?

> **Novelization**
> The conversion of a play, motion picture, or television film into a novel for sale to the general public.
> Generally, novelizations are considered to be a low quality form of literature, just one step above comic books.

2. Have you ever read a novelization? Why, or why not?

Comparing film and novel beginnings – four approaches

Focus on context

1. Did you know the following?

> **Old Trafford:** football ground of Manchester United, a top English football club; the colours of this club are red and white
> **Scholes, Ryan Giggs, David Beckham:** key players for Manchester United some years ago
> **John Motson:** ("Motty") BBC reporter on the *Match of the Day* TV programme
> **Gary Lineker, Alan Hansen, John Barnes:** BBC football presenters on the BBC's *Match of the Day* programme; all are well-known former football professionals

2. View the beginning of the film up to Mrs Bhamra's comment on her daughter. Identify the commentators. What people (do not) need the information in the box to understand the beginning of the film?
3. Now read the novelization (p. 51). What information about the context does it give? What do you think is the target group of the film / the book?

Focus on action

1. View the beginning of the film up to Mrs Bhamra's comment on her daughter. Then in your own words give a short written summary of what happens at the beginning of the film.
2. Would your summary be a good novelization of the beginning of the film? Why, why not?
3. What needs to be added to turn your summary into an effective beginning of a novel which is full of suspense?

Focus on dialogue

1. Read the novelization of the beginning of the film first. Highlight the dialogue.
2. Then view the beginning of the film up to Mrs Bhamra's comment on her daughter. How close is the film dialogue to the dialogue in the novelization?
3. Should the dialogue of a film always be taken over into the novelization? Give reasons for adding, omitting or changing the dialogue.

Focus on feelings

1. How can a director suggest a character's feelings and the atmosphere of a setting? Think of body language, tone of voice, camera operations, music, lighting, slow motion, voice-overs, etc.
2. View the beginning of the film up to Mrs Bhamra's comment on her daughter. Describe the atmosphere in the stadium and the TV studio. How do the characters feel?
3. Highlight all words and phrases in the novelization related to s.o.'s feelings and the atmosphere. Where else in the text would you describe these in more detail?

Chapter One

Old Trafford. Manchester United v. Anderlecht. The crowd a sea of red and white. They're on edge, waiting for the all-important goal.
"But there's a big question mark hanging over Manchester United," John Motson says breathlessly. "Where's the goal going to come from? Will it be Scholes? Could it be Ryan Giggs? Or will David Beckham himself break through?"
The crowd lean forward, urging the players on. The atmosphere is electric.
"Oh, and there's the ball Beckham wanted! Plenty of players in the middle, and Bhamra's making ground as well. It's a decent cross, and there's Bhamra. That's a fine header – AND SHE SCORES!"
The crowd go wild.
"And it's a goal by Jess Bhamra! A superb header, beating the defender and planting the ball just out of reach past the goalkeeper. Jess Bhamra makes a name for herself at Old Trafford! Have we discovered a new star here, Gary?"
Back in the TV studios, Gary Lineker turns to Alan Hansen and John Barnes. They all look well impressed.
"Good question, Motty," says Gary, turning to the panel. "Could Jess Bhamra be the answer to England's prayers, Alan?"
Alan raises his eyebrows. "There is no denying the talent there, Gary. She's quick-thinking, comfortable on the ball, she's got awareness and vision. I tell you what, I wish she was playing for Scotland."
Gary laughs and turns to John Barnes. "John, do you think England have found the player to help them relive our 1966 World Cup glory?"
"No question, Gary," says John. "I think we've finally got the missing piece of the jigsaw. And, the best thing is, she's not even reached her peak yet."
Gary turns to the camera. "Now, joining us in the studio is Jess's mother, Mrs Bhamra."
MUM?! Get out of my fantasy!
"So, Mrs Bhamra, you must be very proud of your daughter?" Gary beams.
"Not at all!" shrieks Mum. "She shouldn't be running around with all these men, showing her bare legs to seventy thousand people. She's bringing shame on her family – " she gives the panel a filthy look " – and you three shouldn't be encouraging her."
Gary, Alan and John look like …

From *Bend it like Beckham* by Narinder Dhami. Reproduced by permission of Hodder and Stoughton Limited.

Annotationen

1 **on edge** nervous
5 **to urge s.o. on** *here*: to shout for the players to attack
6 **to make ground** to move forward
12 **panel** group of experts discussing s.th.
13 **there's no denying the talent** everybody sees the talent
14 **awareness** the ability to notice s.th.
15 **to relive s.th.** to experience s.th. again
17 **jigsaw (puzzle)** picture cut up into pieces that you try to put together again
18 **peak** the highest point
21 **to beam** to smile brightly
23 **shame** *Schande* – **filthy** *here*: angry

A step further

1. Finish the final sentence. What might the presenters look like?
2. In general, are you happy with the novelist's version of the beginning of the film? Why, why not?
3. Where in the text do you learn that it is written from Jess's first-person point of view? Do you think this point of view is a good idea? Why, why not?
4. Write a beginning for a novelization which introduces Jess and her dilemma in a different way but is equally true to the film. The four approaches on page 50 may be useful.

7 years later: conducting a TV show

The context

At the end of *Bend it like Beckham*, Jess and Jules leave their families for America. Imagine that after some time together the two young women go different personal and professional ways and lose sight of each other for some time. After some years, one of them has become the female soccer equivalent to David Beckham whereas the other one has become successful in a very different way. Both are invited to the American TV show "This is your life".

The task

Prepare, rehearse and act out this show, in which the female soccer star describes the story of her soccer career from high school to the present. In between, the presenter welcomes the second woman and other surprise guests from the star's past for an unexpected reunion. The new arrival tells the audience how he / she saw the star and recalls memories and anecdotes. The presenter's role is to keep the show going, to create a pleasant atmosphere and to make his / her guests talk. The guests describe people and events from their perspective, give reasons for their decisions and explain how they felt in certain situations.

Useful phrases for the presenter:

- when talking to the audience:
  Thank you for the warm welcome / the big applause ... I welcome you to a new edition of my favourite TV show...
  My very special guest today – I'm sure you all know him / her – is ... He / she is famous for... Let's give a big round of applause for ....
- when talking to guests:
  It's great that you have found the time to be on my show today ... Please, take a seat and feel at home. Make yourself comfortable. Let's first talk about ... How did you feel / react when ... What was it like when...
  Looking back, would you do anything differently? What would you have done if s.th. had happened?
  If you had the chance to meet X again, how would you feel about this? Well, here is your chance! Let me welcome ...
  It's great having you on my show.

Planning a sequel

The context

A film company is planning a sequel, i.e. a follow-up film, to *Bend it like Beckham*. Which characters would you like to see again in this sequel? Which new characters do you think Jules and Jess will meet in their future lives? Will the two girls go separate ways at some point? What happens in the Bhamra and Parker families during their absence? How about the relationship between Joe and Jess?

The task

In groups of four to five, collect more questions you think a sequel should answer, then develop ideas for this film. In order to convince the film company of your ideas, prepare an attractive "information pack" which is made up of an informative one-page information sheet, a poster or radio ad to advertise your sequel, and a 10-minute group presentation.

Ideas

- Suggest a catchy title.
- Sum up the action in a few sentences. Think of new storylines and topics.
- Explain how the familiar characters develop.
- Draw character profiles of the new characters. Suggest actors / actresses for these roles.
- Outline a possible sequence of scenes (characters, setting, situation / conflict, topic of dialogue) for the first part of the film. Make a grid.
- Describe the first and final scenes of the film in detail. How can you give the necessary information about the first film to new viewers?

1 Make six four-word reviews of the film *Bend it like Beckham.*

Examples: (PRAISE) Fast-paced action – brilliant acting!
(CONTRAST) Memorable moments – unconvincing ending!
(CRITICISM) Unbelievable characters – confusing plot!

four-word reviews

A sixteen-year-old female football fan might say: "..."
A lover of action films could comment: "..."
The president of the Keira Knightley fan club is likely to say: "..."
My parents will probably summarize the film in the following way: "..."
I would sum the film up like this: "..."

excellent	unique	confusing
extraordinary	thrilling	entertaining
brilliant	skilful	unusual
fascinating	exceptional	strange
wonderful	mysterious	unbelievable
terrific	unbeatable	lifelike
entertaining	satisfying	larger-than-life
original	average	fast-paced
plausible	memorable	slow-paced
(un)realistic	surprising	illogical
effective	unexpected	suspenseful
masterful	(un)predictable	gripping
interesting	convincing	disappointing
complex	humorous	boring
	boring	

structure	**message**
action	**editing**
plot	**turning points**
screenplay	**moments**
setting	**ending**
actors	**dialogue**
characters	**humour**
suspense	**effects**
scenes	**images**
emotions	**landscapes**
music	**storytelling**
camerawork	**relationships**

2 How fitting do you find these one-sentence reviews of *Bend it like Beckham*?
Write your own one-sentence review of this film.

one sentence reviews

"Meaningful, good-natured and inspiring, this is precisely the sort of movie that we need during difficult times."

"This film recycles sports movie and culture-clash clichés, running the same gags over and over again."

"It features strong acting and directing, lots of keen observations about what it's like living under two different cultures, and plenty of warm humour and effective drama."

"This is a well-written, funny, heart-warming film with a nice message about being true to your own dreams."

"*Bend It* is a surprisingly smart look at romance, family relationships, and parental expectations."

Before you read

– Do you usually read reviews of new films? Why, or why not?
– To what extent do film reviews influence your decision to see a film in the cinema?

BEND IT LIKE BECKHAM, a film review by Steve Rhodes

Gurinder Chadha's BEND IT LIKE BECKHAM is an ethnic comedy … with a big heart, but a weak script. It is a sports story that skimps badly on the sports action in favour of ethnic humour. It even throws in a little love triangle, but most of the comedic action comes in the tension between an English girl and her parents, who were born in Pakistan. For the parents, even the wearing of the required soccer shorts is scandalous.

Jesminder "Jess" Bhamra (Parminder K. Nagra) is a high school senior who has been playing with the boys in the park for years. No, not that. She is one of the best members of their ad hoc soccer group. Recognized as a budding star by Juliette "Jules" Paxton (Keira Knightley), a member of a real soccer team for girls, Jess is taken by Jules to meet their strikingly handsome coach, Joe (Jonathan Rhys-Meyers). It's obvious from the beginning that Joe's heart will eventually be torn between the two fetching young women, which will cause a rift in Jess and Jules's friendship. Actually, the entire story is obvious and predictable, which is one of its problems. A bigger one, for me, was the jump-cuts and other cinematic techniques used to avoid showing much real soccer, save some random kicks here and there.

Most of the movie, which plays like a sugar-coated confection that you'd find on Disney's cable channel, concerns Jess's protective family and her quiet rebellion against them. Pretending that she has an after-school job, Jess goes to practice and to the games without admitting to her parents what she is up to. In a parallel story thread, Jess's older sister is about to get married, and the wedding is to be a very big event in the local English-Pakistani community.

So are you up for the movie's final exam? Will Jess's parents let her play in the big game that everyone knows will undoubtedly occur near the movie's conclusion? Who will score the winning goal? And what big event will occur at the exact same time? You are so smart. At least the ending does surprise us a bit in its music choice for the big score. I liked Jess and her family, but why did the movie have to be so formulaic and predictable?

Annotations

2 **to skimp** to not spend enough time on s.th.
3 **comedic** humorous
6 **ad hoc** *here:* meeting spontaneously
9 **rift** split, disagreement
10 **jump-cut** a cut in a scene which leaves out some action
11 **save** except
12 **confection** *here:* a film that is not serious or important
14 **story thread** story line
19 **formulaic** conventional, made with ideas that have been used many times before

1. A classmate suggests *Bend it like Beckham* for an English film evening in your school. Basing your answer on the film review you have just read, how would you respond?
2. What do you learn about the characters and the plot of the film?
3. Give headings to the four paragraphs of the review.
4. Find examples of where the reviewer gives his personal opinion. What do you think are his expectations for a "good" film?
5. To what extent do you agree with the opinions expressed in the review?

A film review is a text which does the following:
– it combines information and evaluation,
– it provides a short summary of the film,
– it expresses an opinion as to why someone should or should not go and see the film.

Here is some advice on how to structure a film review:

The **title and lead in** should attract attention.	**Name of the film and a short comment:** *"Chaos Zone" – A chaotic film you will forget as soon as you leave the cinema!*
The **first paragraph** (= introduction) arouses interest and gives basic information.	**You may start with a quotation:** *"Anyone can cook aloo gobi, but who can bend a ball like Beckham?" This statement is made by the protagonist of the film "…" when he / she …* **… or this way:** *If you are looking for a film for next weekend, then be sure to see [name of film]. I've (not) seen a lot of films in my life but this one is a very special one. [name of film]* ***deals with*** */ describes how … / shows … / portrays ….* *The film* ***is set in*** *[place and time of the film]…*
The **following paragraphs** deal with and discuss different aspects of the film.	**Say in the first sentence what this paragraph is about *(topic sentence)*:** *As far as the characters are concerned, you will find it easy to identify with …. He / She changes in the course of the action / surprises the viewer when … / can be characterized as …* *The plot of the film is as follows: … But to find out how the film ends, you will have to view it yourself. …* *The film is full of humorous effects / language: …* *All the cinematic devices used in the film serve a function and achieve their intended effect. …*
The **last paragraph** (= conclusion) sums up the previous comments in a recommendation if the film is worth seeing, and possibly includes a rating.	***To sum up****, I can only* ***strongly recommend*** *this film because it is easy to understand / full of witty dialogue / highly entertaining / never predictable…* *I would* ***certainly advise*** *you to go and see …* *This film is surely* ***worth seeing*** *because of its …* *It is full of strange / unusual / bizarre characters and surprising twists / humorous or memorable moments / …* *If I* ***were asked*** *to rate this film on a scale from zero to ten, I* ***would give*** *it … points.*

These devices are often used by reviewers:

– a mix of formal and informal language
– the description of key scenes from the film
– comparisons with similar films
– comments on the actors' / actresses' performance and the director's work
– rhetorical questions and directly addressing the reader
– key quotes from the film (memorable comments / dialogue)
– references to the target audience and the genre

Now plan your own review of *Bend it like Beckham:*

Which aspects of the film are to be dealt with in which paragraph?
Decide on a sequence of paragraphs and collect ideas / phrases / quotes for each paragraph.
Formulate a catchy title and turn your notes into a structured and coherent text.

Narrative techniques

Action

setting
time: the present, a sunny day
place: the high-tech TV studio at ***Delhi.com*** – the host's room – a noisy, dirty street which is not tarred → *contrast between progress and backwardness in urban India*

plot
Shortly before her wedding, Aditi enters a TV studio where she listens to a live talk show about censorship in the media, hosted by her (married) lover. The highlight of the show is the live performance of a female dubbist of sex films. During the break Aditi surprises her lover in his room, where he is relaxing. On her way back home from the studio in a taxi, Aditi has a discussion with her cousin Ria about arranged marriages.

suspense
Will Aditi phone and keep in touch with her married lover even though she will be married soon?

Characters

appearance
Aditi (the bride): modern clothes, shoulder-length hair
Vikram (Aditi´s lover and talk show host): smart "Western" style suit and tie
guests in the studio: the traditional Indian women wear saris, the men casual "Western" wear
→ *combination of tradition and western influences in modern India*

body language
Indian female dubbist (when speaking a voice from a sex film): tense facial expression → *she feels uneasy, under pressure, ashamed* **vs. Aditi**, who observes the show with obvious interest and plays an active part in her affair by approaching her lover unexpectedly → *no shame, comfortable with her double life, she enjoys intimacy*

communication
non-redundant dialogues during the discussion and in the taxi
→ *familiarize the viewer with / introduce him / her to the basic opposing views in India on globalization, sex / censorship in the media and arranged marriages*

Main function of the scene:
Points out the discrepancy between India's superficial modernity and conservative tradition

Cinematic devices

Camera operations

Mainly medium shots with little camera movement → *emphasis is on the speakers and their dialogues*
Close-ups of faces:
- Aditi and Vikram → *mutual love, passion and longing (extreme close-ups)*
- Aditi and Ria in taxi → *their different points of view are reflected in their facial expressions (justification vs. criticism)*

Extreme close-up of female speaker while dubbing the sex film scene → *shows her disapproval while moaning; her shy, hesitant body language contrasts with her words*

Visual symbols

the props in the TV studio
the universe, a large open eye, etc. → *represent (technological) progress and appeal to the audience to accept globalization*
the poster with one man and five young boys all dressed alike advertising "The good life!" (programme of the satellite television company AirTel)
→ *reminder of the all-pervasive influence of the western media, but also a hint at Aditi's and Ria's shared dream of a happy family life*

Sound effects / film music

permanent blowing of car horns → *conveys a realistic impression of noisy Indian streets*
instrumental Indian music (mixture of modern and traditional elements) when presenting the "top dubbist of Delhi"
→ *musical trademark of the show*

Other effects

lighting: mainly blue light in the studio → *artificial atmosphere*; warm, dimmed light in the host's room
→ *intimate situation*
contrast in terms of settings, characters and viewpoints (the basic structural device in the sequence)

Pre-Viewing tasks

- What comes to your mind when you read the terms "monsoon" and "wedding"?
- Talk about the cover of the video: "The rain is coming ... and so is the family." – What does that mean? What is the film about?

While-viewing tasks

1. View the first three minutes and identify some main characters. How are they involved in the preparations for the wedding?
2. View the TV discussion up to the point when the "dubbist" appears. From then on, turn off the sound for the rest of the sequence. What is the scene about? Write the dialogues between
   - Aditi and the TV show host,
   - Aditi and her older cousin Ria.
3. View the sequence again. Compare your dialogues with the real dialogues in the scene.
4. a) What is the main function of the sequence in the context of the film?
   b) How do the setting, the plot, the characterization and the cinematic devices support this function?
5. Outline further plot developments. What problems may the characters face, and what conflicts might they have to cope with?

Post-viewing activities

Make comparisons with *Bend it like Beckham*:

a) Point out parallels and differences between Aditi / Ria and Jess / Jules in terms of character, views on life, ambitions and constraints.
b) Find scenes in *Bend it like Beckham* which have some similarity to parts of this sequence. Think for example of meetings between lovers and arguments between friends.
c) Compare the culture clash in this scene from *Monsoon Wedding* with the conflict of cultures as presented in *Bend it like Beckham*.

Narrative techniques

Action

setting

place: Chandrapore, India, the local Club
→ *like a small British island in an exotic Indian ocean*
time: late 1920s
Scene 1: at night; Scene 2: in the afternoon, a very sunny day

plot

Dr Azis walks Mrs Moore back to the Club, to which Indians are not admitted. Adela is waiting for her. Both complain that they have not seen the "real" India yet. Therefore Mr Turton suggests organizing a "Bridge Party" to bridge the gulf between East and West. The party takes place on a sunny afternoon. Surprisingly, more people than expected follow the invitation. Mr and Mrs Turton take their guests around to meet the visitors. Both Adela and Mrs Moore are horrified by the occasion.

Characters

appearance

at the "Bridge Party": Mrs Moore, Adela and Mrs Turton wear dresses in light, pastel colours with hats to match; Ronnie and Mr Turton are in very formal three-piece suits, wearing hats; Indian guests are dressed in very bright colourful clothes → *stresses the contrast between the two groups, colours might reflect Mrs Moore's and Adela's view of the country*

use of language / communication

Mrs Turton addresses the Indian ladies who have come to the tea party in Urdu → *underlines her feeling of superiority, she assumes that they do not speak English*
Indian ladies address Mrs Moore in English, they just mention different places in London → *ridicule the British by playing with their expectations*

Main function of the scene:
Illustrates the atmosphere in colonial India

Cinematic devices

Camera operations

Mrs Moore taking leave of Dr Azis:
camera first assumes Azis's point of view when an over-the-shoulder shot shows her face, then he watches her walk away towards the Club; after that the perspective changes with the camera, zooming out on Azis standing at the gate, a small white figure in the darkness
→ *stresses the distance between the two people, but also the attraction she holds for him*

Visual symbols

River Ganges glittering in the moonlight
→ *sacred river, symbol of nature, contrasts with the unnatural world of the Club*
→ *in a wider sense: the river's strength and endurance contrast with the short-lived Empire*

Film music

At the party a band plays three different tunes:
- "Tea for Two"
- "Roses of Picardy"
- "In a Monastery Garden"

→ *pleasant tunes gloss over the tense atmosphere*

National Anthem (God Save the King) played at the end of each scene, everyone dutifully stands up → *stresses the absurdity of the situation*

Other effects

Use of contrasts throughout the scenes:
- Indian musicians play very British tunes
- at the Bridge Party: Indian guests stand on the lawn, British hosts sit on a terrace
- inside (the Club) vs. outside (the real India)
- dark night vs. Azis in bright white clothes

→ *stresses the gulf between the two groups*

Putting the scene in context:

Mrs Moore and Adela Quested, who is engaged to Mrs Moore's son Ronnie, travel to India to visit their son / fiancé, a British magistrate posted in Chandrapore, a small town on the River Ganges. On the train journey from Bombay to Chandrapore, they meet the governor, Mr Turton, and his wife. After a few days in town they complain about not seeing the real India. Thus, when they are at the Club one night watching a show, Mrs Moore wanders off to a mosque, where she meets Dr Aziz, a young Indian doctor, who walks her back to the Club.

Pre-viewing task: Collect information about the British rule in India. Give a two-minute talk in class.

While-viewing tasks

1. Before and during the Bridge Party Mrs Moore, Adela, Ronnie, Mr and Mrs Turton discuss their relationship to the local Indian community. Here are some of the statements you will hear. Who says what? Compare the different attitudes that are reflected in their comments.
   a) They hate it as much as we do.
   b) I don't understand people inviting guests and not treating them properly.
   c) I'm not a missionary or a sentimental socialist.
   d) God has put us on earth to love and help our fellowmen.
   e) We are not out here to be pleasant.
   f) Do you really want to meet the Aryan Brother?
2. Examine the cinematic devices used to stress the gulf between the British and the Indians.

Post-viewing tasks

Watch scenes 29 and 50 (and perhaps 53) from *Bend it like Beckham.* In these scenes you learn something about Mr Bhamra's past. Outline to what extent he has been affected by racial prejudice. Do you think watching this excerpt from *A Passage to India* makes it easier to understand his attitude? Explain why or why not.

Suggestions for further work

- Unlike *Bend it Like Beckham*, this film is based on a novel. The respective excerpt from Forster's novel (see chapter "Mosque II" in the book) could be studied in class to discuss the changes that have been made. A lot of the dialogue in the film scene comes from the novel. There is also interesting material available from http://www.filmeducation.org/filmlib/p.html, which explores in detail the ways in which David Lean has translated E. M. Forster's novel into a film.
- Other interesting films based on novels set in India are *Heat & Dust* or *Staying On.* Students could discuss the question of what it is that makes India so fascinating to novelists / filmmakers. Salman Rushdie takes a critical view on these films in his essay "Outside the Whale", contained in his collection of essays and criticism *Imaginary Homelands* (1991).

Tasks: Solutions

While-viewing

1. a) Mrs Turton; b) Adela ; c) Ronnie; d) Mrs Moore; e) Ronnie; f) Mr Turton
Mrs Moore and Adela are newcomers to India and show a naïve curiosity about the country and its people. They are not affected by feelings of white supremacy. The Turtons and Ronnie, however, who are part of the colonial system, believe it is best to avoid contact as much as possible. Mr Turton's reference to the 'Aryan Brother' is very ironical.

2. Cf. scene profile.

Post-viewing

When Joe calls on the Bhamras to apologize, Mr Bhamra explains why he does not want Jess to dream about a career in soccer. Unlike his wife, who objects for traditional, religious reasons, he is afraid that Jess might be hurt. When he was still at school in Nairobi, he was a top-class bowler and won the East African cup with his team. When he moved to England, however, he discovered that he was denied admission to the English clubs. Later, when he sees how talented Jess is, he admits that he was wrong to give up so quickly and he encourages his daughter to fight for her dream. In the epilogue he is shown playing cricket in front of their house with Teetu and Joe. (Individual answers to Part 2) intermediate level

Course Test No.:	*Course:*	*Name:*	*Date:*

Film scene: *Bend it like Beckham* (2002), (Jess "breaks up" with Joe): 01:35:36 – 01:37:22

Text: Narinder Dhami. *Bend it like Beckham* (2002), Klett edition p. 94.

"Joe! Joe!" I raced across the pitch, holding my sari up with one hand. He was out under the floodlights on his own, juggling a football on his knees. "I'm going! They said I could go!"

At first he looked stunned, then he beamed as I threw myself into his arms and we hugged each other to bits.

"That's brilliant, Jess."

There were a few wolf whistles from some guys on the neighbouring pitch, and I pulled away from him, embarrassed.

"Sorry, I forgot."

"It's OK now, Jess," Joe said quickly. "I'm not your coach any more. We can do what we want."

He reached out to pull me to him again, but I backed away. This was one of the hardest things I'd ever had to do. But I'd thought things through, and it was the only way.

"Joe," I began uncomfortably.

Joe looked behind him, an expression of alarm on his face. "Your dad's not here, is he?"

I shook my head. "I'm sorry, Joe. I can't…"

Joe looked confused and I almost melted, but I forced myself to harden my heart again. "Jess, I thought you wanted –"

"Letting me go is a really big step for my mum and dad." I couldn't look at him. Instead, I reached out and fiddled with the zip of his trackie top. "I don't know how they'd survive if I told them about you too."

There was silence for a moment.

"Well, I guess with you going to America, there's not much point anyway," Joe said bravely. "Is there?"

He was giving me a way out without making it hard for me. I shook my head, and we hugged each other goodbye.

It might be the right decision, but it still hurt. Why couldn't life just be simple and straightforward?

Annotations:

5 **wolf whistle** a loud whistle to express admiration for an attractive woman

13 **to melt** (of ice) to become water

Tasks:

1. *On the basis of both film scene and novelization, briefly describe the situation Jess and Joe find themselves in at this point of the story. Point out what decisions Jess has made and what the main reasons for these decisions are.*

2. *Describe and compare how the protagonists' feelings and the atmosphere are expressed in the film and in the novelization.*

3. *Choose one of the following tasks:*
   a) *After the conversation with Joe, Jess goes home and calls Jules to tell her about the good news and her meeting with Joe. Write their dialogue.*
   b) *After the conversation with Jess, Joe stays at the football pitch and thinks about the news. Write an interior monologue from his perspective.*

Preparation

Comparison of film and novelization with the help of pages 50-51.

Tasks: Solutions

1. a) *Jess and Joe are in love, but her family background and the fact that Joe has been her coach until recently have prevented them from starting a relationship. Jess has been offered a scholarship after her team won the final. Jess has just got her parents' permission to go to the U.S., where she is going to play football at a college (Santa Clara college). In the scene given, which is set on the football pitch, Jess tells Joe about the good news.*
   b) *Jess has made two decisions. Firstly, she has decided to go to the U.S. together with Jules because studying and playing football there will bring her nearer to her greatest dream, i.e. playing football professionally. Secondly, Jess wants to tell Joe that she cannot start a relationship with him. The reason for this decision is that she appreciates her parents' letting her go very much. Her parents are Sikhs and they would never allow a relationship with a non-Sikh man (Joe is Irish). Jess does not want to hurt them by acting against their will and bringing shame on the whole family. Consequently, despite the facts that they love each other, that Joe is not Jess's coach any longer and that Jess leaves her parents' house, a relationship is still not possible.*

2. *FILM:*
At the beginning of the scene: Jess and Joe smile, seem very happy, enthusiastic, they hug each other passionately; when the music stops the essential part of the scene starts: Joe strokes Jess's arms and shoulders, then tries to kiss Jess, but she closes her eyes and backs away → close relationship, but something seems to be wrong; after the rejected kiss: Joe is very irritated, steps back – serious facial expressions, no body contact → emotional and spatial distance; Jess permanently looks into Joe's eyes (→ self-confident, decisive), Joe looks down (→ cannot bear her glare, hurt), then takes her hand and strokes it (→ understands her decision); they agree that a relationship wouldn't make much sense anyway (Jess slightly shakes her head), music starts again to indicate that the decision is definite; they hug each other again, this time rather statically, Jess's eyes are closed; then Jess has got tears in her eyes (→ her decision is not only hard for Joe, but also for herself).
Mainly the use of body language, e.g. facial expressions (camera zooms in to show the characters' faces), the soft, calm music at the beginning and at the end, and the colours (except for Jess's dress cold and artificial colours dominate the scene) help to show the characters' feelings and to create a sad atmosphere.

   NOVELIZATION:
   The characters' feelings are expressed through a description of action and body language; however, the body language is described from Jess's perspective only ("Joe looked confused", l. 13); dialogue predominates, facial expressions are only twice described in detail ("an expression of alarm on his face", l. 11; "I shook my head", ll. 12, 18); the emotional aspect of physical actions is only rarely indicated ("I threw myself into his arms and we hugged each other to bits.", l. 3f; "I backed away", l. 8); due to the role of Jess as first-person narrator, the reader learns about Jess's emotions ("I pulled away from him, embarrassed", l. 5; "I almost melted", l. 13) but has no direct access to Joe's feelings and thoughts.

   Summary: Whereas in the film body language, music and colours implicitly reveal the mood of the situation, the novelization explicitly conveys the characters' feelings through Jess's observations and comments. Thus, the film expresses the character's feelings and the atmosphere in much more detail and complexity than the novelization.

3. *Both dialogue and interior monologue should*
   - *include information about the meeting and comments on Jess's rejection of Joe,*
   - *express Jess's / Joe's feelings (Jess: on the one hand happy because she is going to America to fulfil her dream, on the other hand sad because she has to leave Joe and has probably hurt his feelings; Joe: sad because he hoped for a relationship with Jess but he is also proud of and happy for her),*
   - *fit the characters and the situation in terms of language and tone.*

intermediate level

Course Test No.:	*Course:*	*Name:*	*Date:*

Film scene: *Bend it like Beckham* (2002), Scene 17, 00:23:35 - 00:26:08
(Jess lies to her parents in order to be able to stay with the Harriers.)

Text: Curtis Mayfield, *Move on up*

Move on up

Hush now child, and don't you cry
Your folks might understand you by and by
Move on up towards your destination
You may find from time to time complications
Bite your lip and take a trip
Though there may be wet roads ahead
You cannot slip
So move on up and peace you will find
Into the steeple of beautiful people
Where there's only one kind
So hush now child and don't you cry
Your folks might understand you by and by
So move on up and keep on wishing
Remember your dreams are your only schemes
So keep on pushing
Take nothing less, not even second best
And do not obey, you must have your say
You can pass the test
Move on up, move on up, move on up …

(142 words) *(http://www.lyricskeeper.com/54_soundtrack-lyrics/74198-destinationmove_on_up-lyrics.htm)*

Annotations:
2 **Hush**. Be quiet. – 10 **steeple** a tall tower with a spire on top, rising above the roof of a church – 15 **scheme** plan

Tasks:

1. *Sum up the message of the song and show that it reflects the situation Jess is in at this stage in the film.*

2. *Examine how cinematic devices are used to show that Jess's new, secret life is more exciting than her life at home. Pay special attention to camera operations and the soundtrack (music and lyrics).*

3. *You have a choice here. Do one of the following:*
   a) *In l. 18 the lyrics say "… do not obey, you must have your say". Comment on this statement. Do you think Jess is right to disobey her parents? Why or why not?*
   b) *You know that Jess does not keep a diary, but she confides in Beckham, i.e. she talks to his poster on the wall. Write a monologue in which Jess tells Beckham about her new life as a member of the Hounslow Harriers. Make sure that what you say is in line with what we see in the film.*

Preparation

Film plot:
It is important that students understand Jesminder's dilemma. In the preceding scene (scene 16) her old Indian friend Tony and her new English friend Jules both advise her not to tell her parents the truth but to lie to them. Jess resents having to do this because she feels she does not want to do anything that is morally wrong.

Cinematic devices:
Students should be familiar with camera operations (especially with field sizes and movements) and with film music.

Writing skills:
Students should have some knowledge of the basic structure of comments and should have some command of useful phrases for expressing one's opinion.

Tasks: Solutions

1. The song deals with the difficulties connected with achieving one's dream. The speaker consoles the young addressee ('child') not to despair and encourages him / her to go on fighting for this dream even if his / her family is opposed to it ('your folks'). The speaker tells the addressee to believe in his / her own potential ('you cannot slip'). The general mood is optimistic. Jess could be the person the speaker addresses because she has to battle with her parents in order to realize her dream. As the daughter of a strict Sikh family she is expected to grow up to be a good mother and wife one day. Playing football, which also involves showing your naked legs to hundreds of men, is completely unacceptable.

2. The 'scene' consists of a rapid alternation of very short shots basically revolving around Jess's new life with the Hounslow Harriers. At the beginning we see her leave the house and pick up her sports bag, which is hidden in a flower bed in the front garden. The music sets in when she has got the bag. It is fast and rhythmic.
The camera focuses on Jess's legs. The camera follows her running to the football pitch (tracking shot). The idea of speed / movement is stressed. There is no dialogue in this scene. The lyrics of the song can be considered a substitute for this. They comment approvingly on Jess's decision to follow her dreams. We see her practising with the other girls of the team, enjoying the physical exercise (jumping high into the air, performing cartwheels), celebrating her first goal in a match, fooling around with Jules and Joe. The few shots showing Jess at home, which are interspersed, emphasize the contrast between the two worlds. While her mother is trying to teach her how to cook, she plays football with a cabbage behind her back. Mrs Bhamra has to drag Jess to the stove to stir the Aloo Gobi. The highly motivated, active footballer turns into a reluctant, passive housewife. A static shot of the kitchen with a frying pan in the foreground underlines this impression.

3. a) Individual answers. The comment should have a suitable introduction and conclusion. It should also juxtapose the pros and cons of Jess's decision.
b) Individual answers. The monologues should reflect Jess's feelings of joy and excitement but should also deal with her feelings of guilt.

advanced level

Course Test No.:	*Course:*	*Name:*	*Date:*

Film scene: *Monsoon Wedding* (2001), (Visiting her lover at work): 00:04:44 - 00:08:28
Bride-to-be Aditi listens to a discussion about aspects of old and new ways of Indian culture in a TV studio and then secretly meets her married lover, i.e. the TV show host. On her way back home from the studio, Aditi has a discussion about marriage with her cousin Ria.

Text: Beyond Stereotypes: *Globalization's Winners and Losers* by David H. Wells

Globalization has provoked outrage among conservatives in India with the arrival of satellite television such as Rupert Murdoch's STAR TV, MTV and other foreign channels. India, a nation where cinematic kisses were only recently permitted, was shocked when viewers first encountered kissing, lovemaking and nudity. India was pressed to accept in five years changes that the West slowly accepted over several decades. Particularly in the cities, values, attitudes and behavior are in a state of tremendous flux as sex becomes public. [...] One sad result is that a recent study showed the number of teenage abortions rising by 20 per cent in the space of a year in the southern state of Kerala.[...]
While modernity, according to social theorists, is said to free individuals from existing identities, Indians are especially fearful of the new identities pushing out older ones. India's superficial modernity, exemplified by those who adopt western lifestyles while revering conservative tradition, has created a societal dissonance. India has clearly had a smattering of modernist characteristics yet one would hardly call India modern. Modernity reduces the importance of birth status and increases the value given to education or other merit based achievements. The ability to empathize with and share in another's plight is at the heart of modernity. Lacking it, modernity degenerates to commercialism. While India is slowly putting consumer items into the hands of the masses, whether it is becoming modern is another question.

(236 words) *(http://www.aliciapatterson.org/APF2102/Wells/Wells.html)* Printed by permission

Annotations:
5 **flux** a situation in which things are changing a lot and you cannot be sure what will happen;
9 **to revere s.o. / s.th.** to respect and admire s.o. / s.th. very much – 9 **smattering** a small number;
11 **merit based** deserving praise because of its quality – 11 **plight** a very bad situation that s.o. is in

Tasks:

1. *What image of India do the film scene and the text present?*
2. *Explain how the characters, the settings and the cinematic devices in the film scene from "Monsoon Wedding" serve to show India's situation between modernity and tradition.*
3. *Having just seen this scene from "Monsoon Wedding", you write a letter to a British Internet Youth Magazine, in which you comment on Aditi's dilemma from a German perspective, also considering the wider context of globalization. In your letter, refer to the problem Jess has to cope with in "Bend it Like Beckham".*

Film Scene: Preparation

In general: Make students familiar with narrative / cinematic devices and their functions.
Provide background knowledge about arranged marriages and the status of women in India.
In detail: Watch comparable scenes of *Bend It Like Beckham* which focus on arranged marriages, the role of women and Indian tradition (cf. *Szenenprotokoll*)

Tasks: Solutions

1. *Key words: the arrival of satellite TV (the growing influence of the western media) – sex has become public – conservative clash with liberal views – modernity meets tradition – new trends: teenage abortions, western lifestyles, commercialism – ...*
2. *Cf. scene profile "Monsoon Wedding", p. 56.*
3. *–*